D1371014

FOURTH EDITION

ANSWERING the CALL:

Understanding the Duties, Risks, and Rewards of Corporate Governance

Lynn Shapiro Snyder, Esq.
and Robert D. Reif, Esq.

Created in collaboration with:
EPSTEINBECKERGREEN
www.ebglaw.com
WBL Founding Sponsor

A publication of the Women Business Leaders of
the U.S. Health Care Industry Foundation (WBL)

With Guest Chapter Contributions from:

www.awac.com

K·Fehling
& Associates
People Define Companies
www.kfasearch.com

www.jeanfreeman.com

www.deloitte.com

Snyder, Lynn Shapiro and Reif, Robert D., Esqs.

Answering the Call: Understanding the Duties, Risks, and Rewards of Corporate Governance (4th Edition); Chapter Four by Chmieleski, Susan and Oard, Cynthia; Chapter Seven by Zeoli, Kimberly; Chapter Nine by Fehling, Kathleen; Chapter Ten by Whitley, Eleanor R.; Chapter Eleven by Freeman, Jean.

Includes bibliographical references and index.

ISBN-13: 978-0-9797557-2-9

Printed in the United States of America, Washington, D.C.

Fourth Edition

TABLE OF CONTENTS

FOREWORD TO THE FOURTH EDITION
The History of Answering the Call

The idea for this book arose from discussions with the senior executive women involved with Women Business Leaders of the U.S. Health Care Industry Foundation (WBL).* In 2002, at one of WBL's Annual Summits, we were discussing how—in light of increased scrutiny of corporate governance—we needed better information before we accepted positions as board members for a wide variety of corporations. Of course, we had heard of the Sarbanes-Oxley Act of 2002. And as busy executives, we wanted clear, concise material to inform us of the risks and to remind us of the many rewards of board membership.

Lynn Shapiro Snyder, Esq., founder of WBL, accepted the challenge that would later become this book—which describes the basic information every potential or current board member should know about board membership. To date, over *13,000* copies of this book have been made available to senior executives, directors, and potential directors at health care and non-health care companies around the globe. Its content has benefited both men and women.

We are excited to publish a significantly expanded fourth edition with new contributors. This edition, like the prior editions, is co-authored by Lynn Shapiro Snyder, Esq., founder of WBL and senior health care and life sciences member of Epstein Becker & Green, P.C. (EBG). Joining her as co-author is Robert D. Reif, Esq., Chair of EBG's National Business Law Practice Group and Chair of the Corporate and Transactions subgroup within EBG's health care and life sciences practice. EBG's health care and life sciences practices is one of the largest in the United States.

---

* WBL is a network of over 3,000 senior executive women and women board members doing business in the U.S. health care and life sciences industry. The mission is to have the network help these women improve their businesses and continue to grow professionally through corporate board service. More information is available at www.wbl.org.

Exciting contributors to this fourth edition include:

- Susan Chmieleski and Cynthia Oard, senior executives from Allied World Assurance Company, a D&O insurance firm, who contributed Chapter Four on Risk Management Opportunities;

- Epstein Becker & Green member Lola Miranda Hale who provided contributions towards updating Chapter Six about public company listing requirements;

- Epstein Becker & Green member Jesse Caplan who contributed Chapter Eight about non-profit corporations;

- Kimberly Zeoli, Partner at Deloitte & Touche LLP who contributed Chapter Seven about audit committee requirements;

- Eleanor Whitley of the WBL Foundation contributed Chapter Ten about the value and trends relating to gender diversity in the corporate board room;

- Kathleen Fehling of K. Fehling & Associates, a leading retained search firm in the health care industry, who contributed Chapter Nine that provides information on how the board search process really works—and how candidates can best position themselves, and

- Jean Freeman of Jean Freeman & Associates, a leading governance consulting organization, who contributed Chapter Eleven on best practices to help readers develop a practical to do list once they achieve a coveted board seat.

It is our hope that this fourth edition will help more senior leaders of industry from diverse backgrounds answer the call to board service in a thoughtful, informed, and compliant way.

ACKNOWLEDGEMENTS

WBL sincerely thanks our authors, contributors, and their companies for donating their time, energy, and intellect towards creating the newest edition of this book and for donating all proceeds of this book to support the WBL Foundation. Thank you.

Special thanks go to Kara Kinney Cartwright, Esq., our returning editor from the third edition who did a wonderful job of editing this book from cover to cover. We also thank Caroline Cruz who did the graphic design and layout to make this book so visually appealing!

Further thanks to Julia Loyd, Esq. and Joel Rush, Esq. from Epstein Becker & Green for their legal updates to this edition.

Finally, thanks to Eleanor Whitley, the Executive Director of WBL. Her leadership on this book is greatly appreciated.

Finally, both the publisher and the authors thank the significant number of people who have helped with this endeavor over the years. We greatly appreciate everyone's commitment and contributions to this book and its previous editions.

EXECUTIVE SUMMARY

What are the rewards for serving as an outside director?

Although there often is tangible compensation for an outside directorship, most outside directors will say that the greatest rewards for serving on a board are the intangible benefits that result from having the opportunity to work with the other directors of the company. The other directors are likely to be similarly situated senior people from industry, who may be in a position to improve your current business or facilitate your professional growth. The camaraderie that develops through the board meeting process is very rewarding.

The other reward that directors often mention is the opportunity to help another company improve through your guidance and experiences. There is great personal satisfaction in being able "to advise" instead of "to do" in helping another business prosper.

Then, of course, there often is compensation for a director's time and effort. There may be reimbursement for travel to board meetings. There may be a fee paid for each meeting. There also may be payment in stock or in stock options for agreeing to be a director.

What are some of the risks of serving as an outside director?

As with anything that has significant rewards, there are risks involved in serving as a director. If things go bad, there is risk to reputation. There also is risk of personal liability for situations involving the company and the director. As you will read below, a director may be named in a lawsuit against the company and others. Furthermore, recent legislation and heightened government scrutiny have complicated the risk analysis for certain companies. However, being sued and being held liable are two separate matters. Despite the picture painted by recent headlines, an outside director rarely is held personally liable for anything involving the company unless he or she was personally involved in the wrongful conduct.

Nevertheless, it is not a pleasant thing to be named in a lawsuit and, in light of the fact that the United States is a litigious society, a prospective director needs to know about the risks of potential liability and about risk management tools that can mitigate the effect of lawsuits, such as indemnification and insurance for company directors and officers.

What type of due diligence should you do before accepting a directorship?

It used to be the case that a senior executive who was asked to be on a board was so grateful for the honor that he or she would just say "yes." Those days are over. Just as the company's senior management and current board members go through a due diligence process to determine whether to extend a directorship offer to a particular board candidate, so too should the candidate ask some questions and do some of his or her own investigations to make sure the match is desirable. This is so important, because directorship requires a very close and personal relationship among directors and with senior management with whom there will be a lot of interaction.

Once on the board, what will be expected from you?

Much of this book addresses the topic of what will be expected from you as a director of a company. There are certain duties and responsibilities. The bottom line is that if you decide to become a director and are given the opportunity to do so, then you must take this commitment seriously and fulfill the various fiduciary duties described briefly in this book in compliance with the law.

What Does A Director Need to Know?

1 Why Should a Busy Executive Want to Serve on a Company's Board of Directors?

The pinnacle of business is a company's board of directors or board of trustees. These directors or trustees are given important decision-making responsibilities for the company, its management, and its shareholders. These important decisions take place in any business, large or small. The board of directors should be a strategic asset to any business.

The pool of outside directors from which companies can draw for corporate governance is small. It includes retired senior executives with the time and energy to be an outside director, existing senior management executives from other companies and industries, former politicians and policymakers, and anyone else who the board and management believe will be a valuable resource to the company.

If a company asks, why should you consider "Answering the Call?"

Board service offers an opportunity to raise your profile

In short, serving on a corporate board can expose you to a whole new set of contacts and individuals whom you may not have met in the course of your daily life. In creating this book, WBL interviewed a number of board candidates to get their impressions on board service as a leadership opportunity and the "why" behind serving on a corporate board.

When asked about the value of board service, candidates most frequently responded that board service is an opportunity to advance your network exponentially. Your contacts and your sphere of influence are increased by the relationships you will build with your board colleagues and company management, and the opportunity for them to know you and the work that you do.

WBL Asked: How Has Board Service Benefitted You?

- *Networking, networking, networking.*
- *Expanded my understanding of other organizations, professionals.*
- *Opportunity to translate business initiatives to current work practice.*
- *Worked with smart people on problems outside my field.*
- *Got the chance to have professional growth at the governance level.*
- *Further developed my business and leadership skills.*
- *Has made me a much more effective CEO.*
- *My board memberships have allowed me to brush up on strategic planning skills.*
- *Gave me the opportunity to better understand the dynamics of group decision-making.*
- *Getting satisfaction of doing a good job for someone.*
- *Personal pride to even be asked.*
- *Met bright interesting people.*
- *Community visibility . . . ability to influence change.*
- *Affirmed my desire to contribute beyond my company.*

Board service provides invaluable lessons, making you better at your "day job"

In small companies, the senior management and board are often one and the same. This may blur the role that a person plays in the company. At one point, the person may be acting as management. At other points, the same person may be acting as a director. However, as companies grow, it becomes more likely that the board will be comprised of both inside directors, i.e., senior management, and outside directors. An outside director has challenges different from inside directors whose daily jobs are with the same company.

Annette Watson, Chair of the Board of the Commission for Case Manager Certification, says that being on a non-profit board, especially chairing such a board, has given her "a new understanding and an even better grasp of the differentiation between the board and the chief executive. Serving on a board has made me a better executive."

Says Ginger Graham, CEO of Two Trees Consulting and a board member of companies such as Walgreens, Genomic Health, Inc., and the American Diabetes Association Research Foundation:

> *As a CEO, I encouraged all my direct reports to serve on a comparable company's board. By their involvement, they would better understand the role of the Board, the needs of the Board members, and the challenges to playing an effective and constructive role as a Board member. Especially the CFO, General Counsel, and head of HR benefit from their roles on other company boards. They become more effective at supporting their own company's Board committees such as Audit and Compensation.*

Describing the professional benefits of board membership as follows, Davina Lane, a director of a health care company at the time, summarized her experience:

> *My board experiences provide another dimension to my business life. I have met people in segments of business that I would not have met in the normal course of my own work. I find them stimulating and their ideas force*

11

me to look at issues from different perspectives. Serving on boards has sharpened my skills in areas not used in the ordinary course of my day.

Board service can be personally rewarding and a chance to give back

As a senior management executive, you have spent many years advancing your business and professional objectives. Often, you have sold a product or service and addressed human resource issues. You may have even bought or sold all or part of your business. You recognize that the accumulation of these experiences has value to those operating similar, or even different, businesses. In interviews, WBL Foundation Associates included some of the leadership benefits of board service as follows:

Being given the chance to influence the direction of a company that was experiencing significant market and financial challenges.

Being a director has provided me with great contacts, new knowledge, and above all, the opportunity to make a real contribution.

In describing board service, particularly on the non-profit level, Donna Cryer, CEO of CryerHealth, commented on the new leadership skills one learns as a board member:

Board service in both non-profit and for profit environments has helped strengthen my skills in building peer-to-peer relationships, leading through influence rather than authority

For those interested in one day being CEO, Ginger Graham describes board service as an essential tool in a CEO's arsenal:

Joining a board provided greater insight and perspective on my role as CEO. Sitting "across the table" from the CEO and viewing [the CEO's] effectiveness at managing the board's communications, preparation, and engagement was a great learning exercise for me as a public company CEO.

Diverse candidates have an even greater chance to make a difference

Most people currently serving as board members in U.S. companies are non-minority males. As you will read in this book, diversity in the boardroom has not been achieved to date, despite business advantages to having a diverse board of directors. Therefore, those of you who otherwise qualify to be a director and who are "diverse" board candidates (e.g., female or minority male) should seriously consider embracing directorship opportunities. Those who already enjoy directorships should seriously consider embracing new board candidates who provide increased boardroom diversity. Many women who currently serve on corporate boards have attested to their efforts to encourage the board to consider additional women candidates for both senior management and board openings. In most cases, the boards in question were more than happy to consider such candidates, but having a woman or minority in the boardroom to suggest other women or minorities was crucial.

Board service can pay

In addition to these intangible professional and personal rewards of sitting on a board, directors may obtain tangible financial rewards. According to Spencer Stuart, a retained executive search firm, "The average board retainer in 1986 was just over $20,000. In 2010, it is nearing $80,000."[1]

In its *2009-2010 NACD Director Compensation Survey*, the National Association of Corporate Directors (NACD) reported that the median annual retainer for directors ranged from approximately $20,000 to $30,000 for the smallest public companies across a wide geographic region.[2] Among medium-sized companies ($1B–$2.5B), these numbers jump to a range of $40,000 to $45,000. The range for the largest companies ($10B and up) was $60,000 to $75,000. In addition to annual retainers, board members may receive additional fees to attend meetings, to sit on a committee, and to reimburse travel expenses to and from board meetings. Companies also may offer equity and cash compensation. Equity compensation typically takes the form of stock options, but may include direct grants of stock.[3]

Board service can pay, but you should do your homework in this area. Do not let the pay be a deciding factor in accepting or seeking a corporate board seat.

Look before you leap

Whether a company is for profit or non-profit, public or privately held, large or small, any decision to join a board requires a certain amount of due diligence. Also, each senior executive who is contemplating such a career opportunity should be prepared to satisfy the fiduciary obligations expected from this position.

To quote Dorothy Light and Katie Pushor, in their book *Into the Boardroom,* "the most apparent reward for board service is professional, the most overrated is financial, and the most lasting reward was personal."[4]

As you explore the rest of the chapters, we hope this book will help you in "Answering the Call" in a professionally responsible and rewarding way.

2 | What Are a Director's Duties and Responsibilities?

Board service is—plain and simple—a commitment. In any committed relationship, each party has a responsibility to stay true to the promises of that relationship. In the company-board relationship, board members should be prepared to:

- become educated on the rules that govern the relationship;
- perform to their best abilities in accordance with best practices;
- prepare for, attend, and participate meaningfully at every meeting; and
- uphold their fiduciary duties owed to the company.

What is the role of the board of directors?

First and foremost, the board's role is to promote the best interests of the corporation. Shareholders expect the board to provide general direction for the management of the corporation's business, to be involved in major corporate decisions, and to bear the ultimate responsibility for the company's business and affairs.

What's on the Agenda for a "Typical" Board Meeting?

- Authorizing major corporate actions

- Hiring and evaluating the CEO

- Ensuring effective corporate auditing procedures (including retention of outside auditors)

- Reviewing the effectiveness of major operating and financial plans

- Advising senior management on operations and financial management

- Adopting corporate conduct policies and monitoring corporate compliance

- Conducting a self-evaluation—how effective is the board and its composition?

Boards also may call special meetings to act on important matters such as mergers, acquisitions, major financings, joint ventures, or divestitures.

A corporation's shareholders rely upon board members to ensure that the company meets its responsibilities. Board members have the ultimate power and responsibility to determine the company's success or failure. Board members have a duty to others invested in the company—management, shareholders, lenders, and in some cases, the public.

To keep the board's power and duty in check, states have imposed "fiduciary duties"—or legal responsibilities—on board members.

What is a fiduciary duty?

A fiduciary duty is a legal duty imposed on individuals in positions of trust or confidence. These legal obligations, usually imposed on board members by state statute, case law, or both, require that these individuals, the "fiduciaries," act primarily on behalf of the interests *of the company*. Board members are required to put the company's interests above personal interests, always exhibiting loyalty, honesty, and good faith.

> Directors serving on boards of non-profit corporations also have a fiduciary duty. See Chapter Eight for a discussion of fiduciary duties in the non-profit context.

A board member is expected to act "(1) in good faith and (2) in a manner [he or she] reasonably believes to be in the best interests of the corporation."[5] In legal terms, these two expectations are known as the "fiduciary duty of care" and the "fiduciary duty of loyalty," respectively. Together, these two distinct duties comprise the board member's fiduciary duty.

Part 1: The Duty of Care: What does it mean to act in "good faith?"

The duty of care requires a board member to treat tasks with a certain standard of care. *Specifically, the board member should approach his or her duties with the level of care that another person in a similar position would reasonably believe appropriate in similar situations.*[6]

This means that a board member must be careful, responsible, and thoughtful in the performance of his or her duties. The board member must exercise common sense to make informed decisions.

Surprisingly, some board members overlook this aspect of their duty of care—they do not know anything about the company's industry. While a board member need not be an avowed expert on all facets of the business, one must possess, at the very least, a knowledge base that allows him or her to discern whether an effective reporting system is in place. That reporting system should facilitate board oversight by providing the board with periodic and timely reports of significant corporate developments from management and the company's legal and financial advisors. These reporting processes also should allow a director to evaluate management's performance independently.

Board members may rely on the advice of qualified legal

and financial advisors to fulfill their duty of care.[7] Nonetheless, board members should have a basic understanding of:

Since Congress enacted the Sarbanes-Oxley Act in 2002, companies increasingly are seeking directors with accounting and financial analysis skills. This requirement is often particular to certain board members who serve on the company's audit committee. Nevertheless, all board members may rely on the advice of qualified legal and financial advisors to some extent.[8] See Chapters Five through Seven for a detailed discussion of this topic.

- the principal operational and financial plans, strategies, and objectives of the company, including the operating metrics used to measure the company's performance;

- the results of operations and the financial condition of the company and its significant business segments for recent periods; and

- the standing of the company's significant business segments relative to the company's competitors.

Part 2: The Duty of Loyalty: What does it mean to act in "the best interest of the company?"

As the corporation often is owned either by persons other than management or persons in addition to management, board members must be loyal to the interests of the ultimate stakeholders of the enterprise—the shareholders. A board member must consider this duty of loyalty when faced with differing interests of stakeholder groups, including the employees, suppliers, customers, officers, and community of the corporation. Other corporate officers are required to observe the duty of loyalty also. For example, Delaware courts have extended the duty of loyalty by applying it to individuals not only in their capacity as directors, but as corporate officers as well.[9]

The board serves as the ultimate check that the company is acting in the long-term best interest of the shareholders, although sometimes, in certain circumstances, the board must consider non-shareholder groups, too. No amount of pressure from the media, pleading from company employees, or influence from the CEO who recruited a director should sway that director from his or her primary fiduciary responsibility of loyalty to act in the best interests of the company—and ultimately its shareholders. Moreover, a director owes the duty to all shareholders, and not simply to the subset of shareholders who may have elected that director.

The duty of loyalty also prohibits a board member from using his or her position as a director of the company to make a personal profit or to take other personal advantage, such as by usurping a business opportunity or advantage available to the company. Questions surrounding a board member's duty of loyalty most often arise in situations where there are potential conflicts of interest and/or corporate opportunities. An example: The situation where a board member is on both sides of an issue, such as contemplating the sale of the company to an entity in which that board member has an ownership interest or a competing fiduciary duty. These types of circumstances create "divided loyalty," and conflict with the director's fiduciary duty.[10]

Conflicts of interest and corporate opportunities

A conflict of interest arises when a board member, directly or indirectly, has a financial or personal interest in a contract or transaction brought before the board. A conflict of interest often arises when a director has an interest in another company that the director's company proposes to merge or acquire. Such an interest may exist where the individual sits on both companies' boards, even if the director is not shareholder.

Similarly, if a potential corporate opportunity arises that could benefit either the company or a board member (personally), the duty of loyalty generally provides that board members must make the business opportunity available to the company first. Only after the company has rejected that opportunity may board members pursue it for their own or another's account.

The duty of loyalty does not necessarily forbid transactions that may involve a conflict of interest or corporate opportunity. Instead, the duty of loyalty dictates that board members either refrain from participating in the decision-making process or take other actions to ensure that the board's decision-making process is free from any consideration outside of the company's best interests.

Example of a Conflict of Interest

Kristen is a board member of a coffee dispensing company. The company wants to acquire a paper company so that the coffee company no longer has to purchase paper cups from an outside vendor. In fact, the coffee company is considering acquiring a paper company owned by Kristen.

As a "conflicted" board member, Kristen's duty of loyalty requires that she and the coffee company take certain actions before any decisions are made. After Kristen affirmatively discloses the conflict, the coffee company board may decide to appoint a special committee of disinterested directors to evaluate the transaction independently on behalf of the board.

To avoid conflicts, most companies now require that a certain number of board members be independent of the company. The definition of "independent" varies from company to company, but typically starts with the independent director not being a company employee or a relative of an employee. Indeed, legal requirements for listing on a particular stock exchange may require independent board members under certain circumstances.

To do list: How can a board member fulfill his or her fiduciary duties?

- Attend all board and committee meetings (if appointed to a board committee).
- Participate actively in discussions, ask questions before and during board meetings to understand as fully as possible all potential issues, and vote on matters brought before the board for action.

■ Inquire into potential issues when alerted by circumstances.

■ Discuss matters with the company's legal and financial advisors when necessary to make an informed decision; do not hesitate to employ (or propose that the board employ) the assistance of independent experts on any issue that calls for significant expertise or a second opinion. (Note that directors act as a board and have no individual authority to compel a company to act.)

■ Stay informed by reviewing board and committee meeting agendas and materials in advance of meetings.

■ Assess independence frequently, evaluating whether other board seats or personal or business relationships could affect current and potential transactions; if necessary, inform the board.

■ Stay current by attending educational forums on corporate governance and key industry topics.

■ Get up to speed on industry and company knowledge, by diligently reviewing:

   • All available annual and quarterly reports and press releases;

   • Operational and financial results of the company and its significant business units—this year's, last year's, and far enough back for comfort;

   • Strategic plans (both operational and financial);

   • Operating metrics used to measure the company's performance;

   • The relative standing of the company's significant business segments in relation to the industry competitors; and

   • Risky business areas, and the extent to which the company has an effective corporate compliance program.[11]

To do list: How can a corporate board make sure to address oversight and integrity issues properly?

Similar to the steps set forth above for individual board members to follow, boards, as a whole, also must take steps to ensure corporate compliance. This is especially true because in financially turbulent times, issues of business integrity and compliance become even more crucial to corporate governance.[12] In a 2009 report on ethics and board service, the Conference Board, an economic and business research group, identified five practical steps that boards should undertake to ensure that they properly address integrity issues as part of regular board functions.[13]

(1) Initially, boards should select directors based on objective criteria, with a focus on independence, knowledge and capacity, and business integrity experience.

(2) Companies should manage risk across all levels of the enterprise in which they are engaged. To address these risks, boards should implement an enterprise risk management program that takes advantage of different functional areas of the corporation.

(3) Boards should balance the competing interests relating to incentivizing executives to stay, and monitor benefits and compensation packages.

(4) Boards should maintain oversight of the corporation's ethics and compliance function.

(5) Boards should consult with both internal and external integrity experts.[14]

3 What Are the Risks of Serving on a Board?

A sweeping glance at news headlines shows that board membership does not come without risks. Between corporate scandals and ever-changing rules, board members' duties have come under enhanced focus—as evidenced by the increasing media focus on board actions. These days, board of director membership presents the potential for personal civil, and, where warranted, criminal, liability.

On the other hand, the actual incidence of personal liability resulting in out-of-pocket personal payments by a board member is exceedingly rare.[15] Nevertheless, board members should review a number of failings for which they may be held personally liable.

What laws put board members at risk?

A multitude of laws and regulations put directors at risk. Consequently, a familiarity with these laws is the first step in avoiding personal liability. Directors can be held personally liable for any breach of their fiduciary duties to the corporation, or for any breach of other laws relating to the corporation, its behavior, and its securities. If not careful and diligent, board members can find themselves writing personal checks to the company, its shareholders, or even the government. This chapter outlines some of the different types of laws that fall under a director's purview.

Breach of fiduciary duty: Directors can be held liable to shareholders

A shareholder suit, also known as a "derivative action," is when shareholders sue the corporation as a means of "enforcing the corporation's own rights."[16] Shareholders sue on behalf of the corporation to challenge actions taken by the board. As discussed earlier, board members owe various fiduciary duties to their corporation and to its shareholders. Most shareholder suits are brought by shareholders alleging that board members or officers breached these duties. If a judge or jury finds that a director breached his or her fiduciary duties to the corporation, the director may be personally liable directly to the corporation. This means the director may have to return personally realized profits from any "prohibited transactions" and compensate the corporation for losses.[17]

What can constitute a breach of fiduciary duty? A prime example occurs when a director fails to disclose a conflict of interest, either direct or indirect. A word of caution: Even if a board member acts in good faith and fulfills his or her fiduciary duties, courts will closely scrutinize transactions where board members are self-interested.

Most shareholder actions allege breaches of the duty of loyalty, rather than the duty of care. This is because it is usually much easier to prove that a board member violated the duty of loyalty. To prove a violation of the duty of loyalty, shareholders need only verify that procedures were not followed during a self-interested transaction. Accordingly, the best protection against "duty of loyalty" derivative actions is always following the proper procedures when a board member has a personal or a professional conflict.

In contrast, to determine whether there was a breach of the duty of care, the courts must determine whether a director, in a similar position, would have had a reasonable basis to believe that the action was in the best interests of the company. This legal test is commonly referred to as the "business judgment rule."

The business judgment rule

The same principles that impose fiduciary duties on board members also provide protections. One of these protections is known as the business judgment rule—which comes into play in most cases involving an alleged breach of the duty of loyalty.

Most of the time, before a matter involving board conduct ends up in court, the shareholders must make a demand that the board of directors enforce the corporation's rights that the shareholders would be suing to enforce. In other words, the board must be given an opportunity to heed the shareholders' wishes.[18]

If a matter involving board conduct *does* end up in court, the business judgment rule creates a presumption that (assuming corporate formalities have been met and conflicts of interest are absent) board members fulfilled their fiduciary duty. This means the court initially will presume that board members acted on an informed basis, in good faith, and in honest belief that the action was in the best interests of the corporation. Essentially, if a board decision was incorrect, but in the process of reaching that decision the directors exercised reasonable due diligence under the circumstances, then courts generally will uphold the board's decisions and not hold the directors personally liable. This is the case even where such a decision may have resulted in an unfavorable outcome for the company.

Before finding directors liable for breaching the duty of care, courts will look for evidence that the director's conduct was motivated either by an actual intent to do harm or an intentional disregard of duty. The business judgment rule places the burden of finding that evidence on the shareholders.[19] Even evidence of gross negligence may not be sufficient to support a finding of personal liability against board members.

See Chapter Four for a discussion of how indemnification and insurance address these and other liability risks.

Prospective board members should note that, despite the protection of the business judgment rule, in a very small minority of cases, courts have found board members personally liable for violating their duty of care—when, for example, there was an obvious, prolonged, or egregious failure to diligently participate, oversee, or supervise.[20] As a result of such cases and the consequences suffered by corporations and their shareholders, the United States Sentencing Commission has developed stricter guidelines for effective compliance and ethics programs, and placed significantly greater responsibilities upon boards of directors.[21]

In-Depth Look at the Duty of Care and the Business Judgment Rule

One of the landmark shareholder suits took place in 1996 in the health care industry—*Caremark International Inc. Derivative Litigation.*[22] Caremark shareholders brought an action against the directors of the company after the company pled guilty to criminal charges and paid hundreds of millions of dollars in fines to the federal government for violating health care fraud and abuse laws. The shareholders brought a derivative action against Caremark's board members, alleging that the board members had breached their fiduciary duty of care and therefore should reimburse the company for the fines. The court dismissed the shareholders' derivative claims. In short, the court found that even though the action or inaction of the board of directors may have contributed to the corporation's troubles, the board satisfied its duty of care by, among other things, implementing programs designed to educate employees and adopting internal audit procedures designed to achieve compliance.

In its opinion, the court described the director's role within a company and the limits of a director's personal liability for corporate misdeeds:

> *[The Court is] of the view that a director's obligation includes a duty to attempt in good faith to assure that a corporate information and reporting system, which the board concludes is adequate, exists, and that failure to do so under some circumstances may, in theory at least, render a director [personally] liable for losses caused by noncompliance with applicable legal standards. . . .*[23]

continues

In-Depth Look at the Duty of Care and the Business Judgment Rule

continued

Obviously the level of detail that is appropriate for such an information system is a question of business judgment.[24]

But it is important that the board exercise a good faith judgment that the corporation's information and reporting system is in concept and design adequate to assure the board that appropriate information will come to its attention in a timely manner as a matter of ordinary operations, so that it may satisfy its [monitoring] responsibility.[25]

The liability that eventuated in this instance was huge. But the fact that it resulted from a violation of criminal law alone does not create a breach of fiduciary duty by directors. The record at this stage does not support the conclusion that the [director] defendants either lacked good faith in the exercise of their monitoring responsibilities or consciously permitted a known violation of law by the corporation to occur.[26]

In the wake of *Caremark*, a rigorous corporate compliance program has become one of the best risk management tools against director personal liability. This is especially important in today's tumultuous economic times, when shareholder derivative suits are likely to allege breaches of the *Caremark* duty for directors of distressed companies.[27] Specifically, directors could be found in breach of their fiduciary duties for failing to implement appropriate oversight systems, or missing warning signs of risk. However, there are some hurdles to bringing such claims that offer directors some protection. First, claimants have to prove bad faith on the director's part in order to bring a successful case for oversight liability.[28] Moreover, mere business risks, even those that result in significant losses, are not enough to establish bad faith.[29]

continues

In-Depth Look at the Duty of Care and the Business Judgment Rule

continued

Although bad faith may be difficult to prove, directors still should implement robust risk management and oversight systems to ensure they are satisfying their *Caremark* duties. In 2005, the highly publicized Walt Disney Company shareholder derivative litigation[30] placed the business judgment rule back in the spotlight. In *Walt Disney*, the Delaware Chancery Court evaluated directors' responsibilities with respect to executive compensation decisions. The shareholders questioned the board's processes and decisions related to hiring Michael Ovitz as president, claiming that the enormous severance package Mr. Ovitz received upon termination of his short, and by all accounts extremely disappointing, tenure resulted from directors' and officers' inactions and conflicts of interest. The shareholders argued that the alleged misconduct constituted a breach of these directors' and officers' duties of good faith and loyalty.

While the court found that many aspects of the directors' conduct fell significantly short of corporate best practices (and offered some potential best practices), the court found that the directors had *not* breached their fiduciary duties of good faith and loyalty. Significantly, the decision specifies that, even where a director may have been negligent, the director remains protected by the business judgment rule because, as previously mentioned, the business judgment rule presumes that directors act in good faith. To illustrate, the court established several categories of behavior that may constitute bad faith, namely:

(1) conduct motivated by an actual intent to do harm;

(2) actions that are grossly negligent, accompanied by certain aggravating factors (noting that gross negligence, alone, may not be sufficient to establish a breach of the fiduciary duty of good faith); or

(3) conduct demonstrating an intentional disregard for duty.[31]

While various cases have touched on the *Disney* case since 2005, the law has remained largely intact and has not been significantly affected or overruled.

An In-Depth Look at Securities Laws: The 1933 Act and the 1934 Act

The Securities Act of 1933 was signed into law by President Franklin Delano Roosevelt, partly in response to the stock market crash of 1929. The law's two objectives are:

(1) "to be sure that all pertinent financial and other company information makes its way to the consumer, or potential consumer (the stock owner); and

(2) to prevent misrepresentation and other fraud in the sale of securities."[32]

In 1934, Congress established the Securities and Exchange Commission (SEC) with the enactment of the Securities Exchange Act of 1934. The 1934 Act gave the SEC authority to regulate, discipline, and oversee "all aspects of the securities industry," including "brokerage firms, transfer agents, clearing agencies, as well as the nation's securities self regulatory organizations (SROs)."[33] SROs include the different stock exchanges (e.g., the New York Stock Exchange) and those companies that operate them (e.g., the National Association of Securities Dealers, which operates NASDAQ).

The 1934 Act gave the SEC power to regulate certain company behavior, and to "require periodic reporting by companies with publicly traded securities."[34] The reporting takes place via Form 10-Ks (the Annual Reports), Form 10-Qs (the Quarterly Reports), and Form 8-Ks (the Significant Event Reports), among others.

Both the 1933 Act and the 1934 Act have provisions relating to the obligations of directors. These provisions primarily focus on director stock ownership and disclosure. The liability exposure of a board member under a particular securities law can depend upon whether the board member is an inside or outside director, the degree of control over the corporation exercised by the board member, and whether the board member owns stock in the corporation.[35] Thus, where a director owns stock, the greater the hands-on role of the director (as an insider rather than disinterested director), the greater the risk.

Securities laws: Directors must report individual investments (Section 16)

It is not a conflict of interest, but rather a best practice, for a board member to own securities of that board's company.[36] Once a director owns the company's securities, however, he or she is then responsible for complying with securities laws. (This applies to both private and public companies.)

Directors who own securities in public companies are subject to additional rules. Section 16 of the Securities Exchange Act of 1934 was designed to expose insider trading. The concept behind Section 16 was that a select group of insiders would be privy to important, non-public information by the very nature of their positions, and so Section 16 sought to "take the profits out of a class of transactions in which the possibility of abuse was believed to be intolerably great."[37]

Accordingly, Section 16 requires directors of a public company to report their holdings periodically and to report all trades. Sometimes, Section 16 requires directors to return "short swing" profits to the company (i.e., profits derived simply because of the timing between a sale and a purchase). The Sarbanes-Oxley Act of 2002 has shortened the timeframes for reporting certain acts under Section 16.[38]

As Section 16 has been a newsworthy and notorious governance pitfall, potential directors may be wondering whether they can purchase directors & officers (D&O) insurance policies against the costs and exposure relating to various violations of these laws. This is not the case with respect to suspected violations of the federal securities laws. Usually, companies are not allowed, by law, to indemnify directors against securities law violations.[40] See Chapter Four for a detailed discussion of D&O policies.

In addition to returning short swing profits, board members can be held personally liable for violations of Section 16. If the SEC or a court finds that a director has disclosed non-public information or has used such information improperly, a director may be:

(1) required to pay civil penalties,

(2) banned from further service on public company boards, and

(3) subject to criminal sanction, including serving a prison term.[39]

Although companies generally help their directors and officers comply with Section 16, compliance is ultimately the director's responsibility. Accordingly, directors should seek assistance to ensure compliance, possibly including obtaining outside legal advice.

Securities laws: Directors must report corporate information

In addition to shedding light on individual investments, securities laws are aimed at ensuring accurate and proper disclosure of information about the corporation. This concept goes back to the origins of the 1933 Act and the 1934 Act where, in the wake of the stock market crash and on the heels of prevalent securities fraud in the 1920s, Congress adopted a system that requires companies to disclose all the necessary information in an organized format, so that individual investors can draw their own conclusions on the merits of any particular investment. This system of "full disclosure" to the investors was reinforced by the Sarbanes-Oxley Act of 2002 (SOX).

Board members can protect against personal liability under securities disclosure laws in several ways. The SEC or a court typically will not hold a board member liable for violations involving disclosures if the member can prove that, after reasonable investigation, he or she had no reason to believe that the company made a false or improper disclosure.[41] The more diligent a director is in making sure that the proper information reaches the public, the less likely it is that the director will face liability for the company's failing to disclose material information.

Examples of diligence may include:

- avoiding conflict of interests;

- becoming and remaining educated about the company;

- making sure the reporting systems are working; and

- challenging management.

The 2010 Dodd-Frank Wall Street Reform and Consumer Protection Act (the Dodd-Frank Act, described below) created additional shareholder communication requirements, and authorized a number of new voting rights for shareholders (although some are non-binding votes) with a principal focus on executive compensation—going beyond the Sarbanes-Oxley Act.[42]

Financial Reform: The Dodd-Frank Wall Street Reform and Consumer Protection Act

On July 21, 2010, President Obama signed the Dodd-Frank Act,[43] a financial services industry reform bill that imposes some of the most broadly sweeping requirements on financial institutions since the New Deal legislation arising from the Great Depression. Although the Dodd-Frank Act greatly affects the financial services industry, its impact will be felt much more broadly because many of its corporate governance and executive compensation requirements apply to all public companies. Like SOX, the Dodd-Frank Act may establish, in the future, corporate best practices.

The Dodd-Frank Act creates a number of new powers and responsibilities for the SEC. In particular, the Dodd-Frank Act grants the SEC wide discretion to implement regulations.[44] SEC Chairman Mary Schapiro stated in her related testimony that much of the SEC's upcoming activities would be consumed by rulemaking arising from the Dodd-Frank Act.[45] The governance provisions in the regulations implementing the Dodd-Frank Act should be of particular interest to corporate boards. Overall Dodd-Frank Act themes include increased transparency and enhanced shareholder involvement. For a more detailed summary of the Dodd-Frank Act, see http://banking.senate.gov/public/_files/070110_Dodd_Frank_ Wall_Street_Reform_comprehensive_summary_Final.pdf.

Increased requirements for shareholder communications

While the Dodd-Frank Act does not directly subject the director to enhanced risks for serving on a company's board, this new law highlights a growing trend to increase shareholder involvement in governance oversight. All directors need to be aware of this trend. This new law creates greater scrutiny of board actions by actively engaged shareholders seeking to challenge corporate actions, particularly in the area of compensation and corporate compliance.

The Dodd-Frank Act granted the SEC the authority to create rules (affecting all public companies) giving shareholders access to the proxy process for director nominations. In the past, "few shareholders nominated their own director candidates because of the high costs of soliciting proxies."[46]

The new law will result in more "shareholder candidates" on the nominating list, competing with the board's proposed candidates. This is especially the case where the shareholders are unhappy with the performance of the company or its board. The Dodd-Frank Act also requires boards to share information about the compensation committee with shareholders, and establishes new standards for compensation committee independence.[47]

Other areas where shareholders receive non-binding voting rights will include executive compensation, including golden parachutes (pay for departing executives after a merger or acquisition). However, the law does allow for exemptions from these votes, based on the SEC's evaluation of considerations such as the potential for a disproportionate burden on small companies.[48] Other new disclosure/corporate information sharing requirements that are particularly relevant to compensation will be discussed in the sections that follow.

Securities laws: Public companies must report compensation, board structure, and risk oversight information

In late 2009, the SEC approved enhanced disclosure rules meant to increase investor awareness of the leadership within public companies.[49] Specifically, the 2010 Rules (2010 Rules) were created to increase available information so that shareholders would be better able to evaluate corporate governance issues.[50] Additionally, the Dodd-Frank Act adds several new leadership and compensation disclosure requirements for public companies. In general, the new landscape requires that companies release information related to executive compensation, board structure (governance and director qualifications), and risk oversight.[51]

Compensation

The 2010 Rules require disclosure about the public company's compensation policies and practices for all employees—not just executive officers—if the policies and practices create risks that are reasonably likely to have a material adverse effect on the company.[52] The SEC released a non-exclusive list of situations that could potentially trigger disclosure. The compensation policies and practices that may bear upon the public company's risk management include those compensation policies:

- at a unit of the company that carries a significant portion of the risk profile,
- at a unit within the company with a different compensation structure than the rest of the company,
- in a significantly more profitable unit, or
- in a unit where the compensation expense represents a high percentage of the unit's revenues.[53]

Additionally, the Dodd-Frank Act implemented a "say on pay" provision. Under the Dodd-Frank Act, public companies will be required to provide regular disclosures (in proxy statements) of executive compensation. Indeed, the Dodd-Frank Act requires a separate resolution, subject to shareholder vote, to approve such compensation.[54] Furthermore, the Dodd-Frank Act calls for public companies to disclose executive pay relative to the company's profits.[55] As is the case with the new nomination proxy access requirements, the SEC may create exemptions for smaller companies.[56]

Under the Dodd-Frank Act, public companies will be required to have a policy to "take back executive compensation if it was based on inaccurate financial statements that [do not] comply with accounting standards."[57] This is a significant bolstering of the "return the pay" requirements in effect under SOX.

Finally, the Dodd-Frank Act empowers compensation committees of public companies with new and stronger standards for committee independence, by establishing compensation committee authority to hire any outside consultants needed to bolster the "case" for determining appropriate executive compensation.

Board structure

Both the 2010 Rules and the Dodd-Frank Act require public companies to provide information about the board leadership structure and the board's role in risk oversight.[58] In explaining its purpose behind these 2010 Rules, the SEC observed that disclosure of a company's board leadership structure and the reasons the company believes its structure is appropriate will increase transparency and enhance investor knowledge of how boards function.[59]

Further, the Dodd-Frank Act requires the SEC to promulgate new rules to require public companies to disclose, in their annual reports, the reasons why either the same person(s) will serve as chairman of the board and CEO (or in equivalent positions) or why different individuals would serve these two roles.[60]

The 2010 Rules also address new nominees for the board of directors. In a precursor to Dodd-Frank Act requirements about the proxy nomination access, the SEC requires boards now to disclose:

- "experience, qualifications, attributes or skills that led" to director election;
- any other seats the board member holds (or has held during the past five years); and
- any legal actions (current or past) against each nominee.[61]

The 2010 Rules also require the board to report on the role of diversity in director selection, the first such SEC requirement ever adopted. The board must disclose whether diversity was a consideration in the director selection process. If a diversity policy exists, details about this policy must be disclosed, including how the policy is implemented and evaluated. The role of diversity is discussed in further detail in Chapter Ten of this book.

Risk oversight

The 2010 Rules aim to increase investor awareness of risk oversight by requiring disclosure of the board's role in this important goal. Relevant risks contemplated by the 2010 Rules include those related to investments, compliance, and valuation. While they do not directly alter a director's current fiduciary duties, these new disclosure requirements about the board's role in risk oversight highlight the importance of directors' exercising these duties in key governance matters, namely compensation and corporate compliance.

New Disclosure Requirements

These new disclosure requirements about compensation, board structure, and risk oversight – as a best practice – may well lead to additional challenges to board action. To minimize potential exposure, directors likely will want more emphasis and resources dedicated to compensation decision-making and corporate compliance. A major portion of the Dodd-Frank Act is dedicated to financial institutions, addressing systemic risks – the risk of collapse of an entire financial market, or the "system" as a whole. While this definitely will affect financial institutions, it is too soon to determine whether companies in other industries will adopt the systemic risk management requirements currently found in the Dodd-Frank Act for financial institutions.

Laws concerning dividend payments: Directors must lawfully distribute payments

Directors comprise the governing body that authorizes dividend payments by the corporation. Directors may be found personally liable if they approve a distribution of dividends that is in violation of the company's articles of incorporation, is in violation of legal limits placed upon dividend distribution, or makes a company insolvent.[63] Before declaring a dividend, directors may want to determine whether in-house legal counsel,

financial officers, and ultimately the audit committee have reviewed all applicable laws and governing documents, as well
as the corporation's financial statements. Directors should
note, however, that they "cannot escape personal liability . . .
by delegating to an executive committee the discretion to
declare dividends."[64]

Environmental laws: Directors must be alert to corporate compliance

As shareholders and communities become increasingly
knowledgeable and sophisticated in their understanding of environmental compliance, board members should consider their
role in this regard. Two primary sources of environmental regulation are the Clean Water Act of 1972[65] and the "Superfund"
law (CERCLA), enacted in 1980.[66] These statutes generated a
significant increase in federal and state regulation of activities
that affect the environment, as well as a greater emphasis on
board members' role in corporate environmental violations.
While most environmental laws make some type of direct participation by board members a prerequisite to liability, courts
increasingly are willing to hold board members both civilly and
criminally liable for violations. However, board members must
participate actively by "having directed, ordered, ratified,
approved, consented, or sanctioned the conduct."[67]

Authorizing a "cover-up" also may result in director
liability—maybe not under the realm of environmental law,
but under another aspect of fiduciary duty, such as securities
law. An example of this applied to the directors of Exxon.
Board members were not sued directly under environmental
laws for the Valdez spill, but they did face several securities
claims alleging that they were responsible for related cover-ups.

Tax laws: Directors must be sure the corporation complies

Tax law is another area where directors must be diligent
in ensuring the corporation's compliance. Board members are
liable for penalties related to failure to pay both Federal
Insurance Contributions Act (FICA) monies and federal income
withholding taxes of a corporation.[68] One way to monitor
compliance in this area is to request frequent company reports
on the timely payment of these taxes. In the case of a non-profit

corporation, directors who approve an "excess benefit" transaction and who have not satisfied the requirements for the "rebuttable presumption of reasonableness" of such transactions may be subject to excise tax penalties.[69] See Chapter Eight for more detail on these standards for non-profit corporations.

Privacy laws: Directors of corporations that handle Protected Health Information (PHI) must ensure compliance

Although the privacy and security elements of the Health Insurance Portability and Accountability Act (HIPAA) previously focused primarily on health care entities, recent expansions of the privacy and security rules apply to non-health care entities as well. As part of the far-reaching American Recovery and Reinvestment Act of 2009 (Recovery Act), the Health Information Technology for Economic and Clinical Health Act (HITECH Act) provides for several expansions to HIPAA's original privacy and security elements.[70] Initially, HIPAA required "covered entities," defined as health care providers, plans, and clearinghouses,[71] to take steps to protect personal health information (PHI).[72] Now, under the HITECH Act expansions, "business associates" also are subject to similar requirements. The term "business associate" can apply to many types of corporations, as it includes entities that perform services for a covered entity that involve the use or disclosure of PHI.

For example, business associate services can be professional in nature, such as legal, accounting, or actuarial services. They also can include even broader categories of services, such as consulting, data aggregation, managerial, administrative, and financial services.[73] Under the HITECH Act, the HIPAA security rules apply to business associates, which is a significant shift in the law because, as of February 2010, many types of corporations must put in place reasonable administrative, physical, and technical safeguards to protect PHI—and must have written policies and procedures that document such safeguards. It is too soon to tell how this law will impact a director's duties. Because corporate compliance is an integral part of a director's duties, directors should confirm with management that the company is in compliance with these laws if the company comes in contact with personal health information.

ERISA: Directors must take fiduciary responsibility for benefits administration

The Employee Retirement Income Security Act of 1974 (ERISA)[74] "is a federal law that sets minimum standards for most voluntarily established pension, and health and welfare plans in private industry to provide protection for individuals who are beneficiaries of or participants in these plans."[75] The law establishes responsibilities for anyone who has discretionary authority over ERISA benefit plans—and this may include board members.[76] Breaches of a board member's duties under ERISA may create personal liability—directors may be required to pay back the ERISA plan, or face criminal penalties.[77] Any director agreeing to take on ERISA plan-related responsibility should seek counsel and guidance on all of ERISA's complex rules, and the associated duties and obligations.

Foreign Corrupt Practices Act: Directors must focus on anti-bribery issues, policies, and compliance

The Foreign Corrupt Practices Act of 1977 (FCPA) contains two types of provisions: (1) anti-bribery provisions,[78] which prohibit corrupt payments to foreign officials for the purpose of obtaining or retaining business or securing any improper advantage; and (2) accounting provisions,[79] which require companies with securities listed on any stock exchange in the United States to maintain accurate books and records and an effective system of internal controls. Criminal and civil penalties for violating the FCPA can be severe for companies as well as for individual directors, officers, employees, and agents. Penalties include significant monetary fines and imprisonment.[80] Recent developments and statements from the Department of Justice (DOJ) make clear that the DOJ is increasingly targeting individuals in FCPA investigations, and that potential FCPA exposure reaches all the way to a company's board.

As discussed earlier, *Caremark* established a baseline for corporate governance responsibilities. That case outlines that a board's duty of care to the company requires directors to ensure that the company's information and reporting system (i.e., its corporate compliance program) is adequate, both in concept and design, to assure the board that appropriate information will come to its attention in a timely manner in the ordinary course of operations. This task is most commonly satisfied by developing and implementing an effective corporate compliance program as described in the U.S. Sentencing Guidelines. As part of a company's overall corporate compliance program, it is critically important for directors to take an active role in ensuring that the company's corporate compliance program has a FCPA component, if applicable. In exercising active oversight over the compliance program, directors should require periodic reports to the board on the effectiveness of the FCPA component.

Can directors go to jail?

In an article published by *Corporate Board Member*, John R. Engen interviewed several legal experts about whether directors realistically would be facing the possibility of actual jail time in the wake of all the enforcement activity resulting from highly publicized corporate scandals monopolizing the headlines at that time.[81] Mr. Engen reported that Stephen Cutler, then the SEC's enforcement director, told securities lawyers that he was eager to "heighten the personal accountability of officers and directors who elect to place their own interests ahead of those of the company and its shareholders."[82]

Despite these fighting words from the then SEC chief enforcement officer, legal experts reported that the likelihood that an outside director will actually go to jail for misconduct "are virtually nil." The jail time reported in the media often relates to officers who also are inside directors, i.e., part of the management team. A white-collar criminal defense attorney interviewed by Mr. Engen reinforced this view by stating that, in his opinion, "criminal responsibility is personal," and "unless an independent director is personally involved in the illegal activity, they won't be charged."[83]

Although enforcement actions against outside directors have been relatively rare, a recent enforcement action in 2010 against an outside director suggests that the SEC is beginning to take a more active enforcement approach towards outside directors.[84] The SEC charged a company's former audit committee chairman for enabling the company's CEO to implement a fraudulent scheme involving misuse of corporate funds.[85] Specifically, the SEC alleged that, as a member of the board of directors and chairman of the audit committee, the defendant directly and indirectly violated the Exchange Acts when he became aware of certain red flags but failed to take appropriate action.[86]

Criminal charges require proof beyond a reasonable doubt, which is a difficult evidentiary standard for a prosecutor to meet. This may be one of the reasons why so few people go to jail for Exchange Act violations. TRAC, a tracking service operated by Syracuse University, reported that from 1992 through 2001, only approximately one third of the 609 potential cases referred to Department of Justice by the SEC were actually prosecuted and, of those, only 87 defendants ended up serving jail time.[87]

The Corporate Fraud Task Force, established by President Bush in 2002, had the mission of investigating corporate fraud, including directors' violations of the duty of care and duty of loyalty. As charges have been brought, however, many of these criminal cases have fallen apart.[88] More often than jail time, the criminal indictments of directors have led to large financial settlements.

Although the initial Corporate Fraud Task Force efforts may not have resulted in significant criminal enforcement, early initiatives of the Obama Administration suggest more activity to come in this area. Specifically, on November 17, 2009, President Obama issued an Executive Order establishing an interagency Financial Fraud Enforcement Task Force (Obama Task Force)[89] to replace the earlier Corporate Fraud Task Force.[90] The Obama Task Force varies from and expands upon the former task force in two main ways.[91] First, its creation by Executive Order demonstrates the Obama Administration's dedication to strengthening efforts to combat corporate fraud.[92] Second, the Obama Task Force is comprised of representatives from several federal agencies.[93] According to SEC Chairman Mary Schapiro, the multi-agency approach is significant because "[m]any financial frauds are complicated puzzles that require painstaking efforts to piece together. By formally coordinating our efforts, we will be better able to identify the pieces, assemble the puzzle and put an end to the fraud."[94]

The Obama Task Force already has identified four key areas

of focus. These may serve as some guidance for corporate entities that wish to address these issues internally, and thus minimize the likelihood of a federal multi-agency investigation.[95] U.S. Attorney General Eric Holder stated that the Obama Task Force will focus specifically on the following key types of financial crime:

(1) mortgage fraud;

(2) securities fraud;

(3) Recovery Act[96] and rescue fraud (meaning the theft of federal stimulus funds and the illegal use of tax dollars meant to assist financial institutions); and

(4) financial discrimination (including predatory lending practices).[97]

What is the risk for out-of-pocket director liability?

Unfortunately, there is no simple way to track directors' personal liability payments that are not otherwise reimbursed (such as by D&O insurance or under general indemnification rights against the corporation). However, in a *Stanford Law Review* article, three law professors conducted a comprehensive empirical study of the incidence and amount of out-of-pocket liability imposed on outside directors. The authors reviewed news stories, case law, and professional and business journals. They made hundreds of phone call interviews to law firm attorneys, in-house attorneys, D&O insurers, and current and former SEC officials to collect data for the period from 1980 through the end of 2005.[98] The study found lawsuits common and trials unusual. As for the cases that settled, the article found that "plaintiffs often recover cash, but the cash nearly always comes from the company, a D&O insurer, a major shareholder or another third party. Outside directors make personal payments in a *tiny* percentage of cases"—thirteen to be exact.[99]

These findings make a very strong case that, without willful and knowing improper conduct on the part of a director, directors are not likely to have out-of-pocket liability—even where they are personally liable. Specifically, the authors found:

*[I]f a company has a D&O policy with appropriate cover-
age and sensible limits, outside directors will be potentially
liable to out-of-pocket liability only when (1) the company
is insolvent and the expected damage award exceeds those
limits, (2) the case includes a substantial claim under section
11 of the Securities Act [of 1933, relating to false registration statements] or an unusually strong section 10(b) claim
[under the Securities Exchange Act of 1934, relating to
material misstatements or omissions of material facts or
other "fraud" in connection with the purchase or sale of
securities], **and** (3) there is an alignment between outside
directors' or other defendants, culpability and their wealth.
Absent facts that fit or approach this "perfect-storm"
scenario, directors with state-of-the-art insurance policies
face little out-of-pocket liability risk, and, even in a per-
fect storm, they may not face out of pocket liability.*[100]

Enterprise Risk Management

Enterprise risk management (ERM) refers to the practice
of having corporate management identify, assess, prioritize, and
strategize risks affecting the current and future performance
of an organization or company.[101] In part, the development
of ERM has been a reaction to the high-profile corporate
scandals of recent years.[102] Although ERM is considered a
relatively new concept,[103] ERM has developed as a meaningful tool to control an organization's exposure to various
types of compliance, business, technology, and reputation
risks.[104] The Committee of Sponsoring Organizations (COSO)
of the Treadway Commission has created a framework to assist health care providers, in particular, in improving their risk
assessment practices.[105] As part of the framework, COSO has
set forth four categories of business objectives to assist organizations in establishing an effective risk control environment:[106]

(1) Strategic—this area refers to high-level goals, those
    aligned with and supporting the organization's mission,

continues

Enterprise Risk Management

continued

(2) Operations—this category includes effective and efficient use of the organization's resources,

(3) Reporting—Boards must ensure the reliability of reporting across the organization, and

(4) Compliance—Boards must maintain an effective compliance program with applicable laws and regulations.[107]

See also Chapter Two relating to board duties and corporate compliance programs and Chapter Seven for more on the audit committee's responsibilities relating to Enterprise Risk Management.

In sum: How can directors best counter the risk?

The best way for directors to counter these liability risks is to be a conscientious director. Directors who pay attention to board proceedings, who ask questions of the management of the company in appropriate circumstances, and who generally follow best practices will decrease the chances, if not eliminate the possibility, of *"having the big job land [them] in the big house."*[108]

The real risk to a conscientious director serving a board that becomes embroiled in a lawsuit or a company involved in a scandal is not the possible dollars out-of-pocket, but, more significantly, the potential "time, aggravation and potential harm to reputation that a lawsuit can entail."[109]

To mitigate that risk, which is real and distinct, a director need only perform the requisite due diligence on a company before agreeing to serve on its board. Once there, a director should insist that the board follow and embrace as many of the best practices as is practicable and reasonable for the particular company and the particular board. For a detailed discussion of the due diligence techniques and current best practices for boards, see Chapter Eleven.

4 How Can Directors Manage the Risk of Liability?

GUEST CHAPTER AUTHORS:
Susan Chmieleski, Senior Vice President, Global Risk
Management and Loss Control Lead, AWAC Services,
and **Cynthia Oard,** Senior Vice President,
Allied World Assurance Company, US*

As described earlier, directors may be subject to personal liability under a wide array of laws. In light of this fact and to promote individual board service, most states' laws permit companies to adopt charter provisions that limit a board member's personal liability for his or her corporate board service—through indemnification against specified legal exposures. Companies also commonly procure D&O insurance to provide additional protection when the company's funds are not adequate to provide the financial protection allowed under state law or charter indemnification provisions.

Indemnification provisions and D&O insurance policies come in innumerable variations and provide varying degrees of protection. Before accepting any board position, a candidate should scrupulously review both to ensure sufficient protection. Thoughtfully crafted indemnification provisions combined with a comprehensive D&O policy can go a long way towards insulating a director from using personal assets to pay a judgment in a lawsuit or government settlement.

---

*The opinions in this chapter represent those of Guest Chapter Authors Susan Chmieleski and Cynthia Oard. They do not necessarily represent the opinions of Allied World Assurance Company or the publisher.

Indemnification

Although state laws vary, both the Model Business Corporation Act and the Delaware General Corporation Law allow companies to eliminate or limit—indemnify—a director's personal liabilities to the company or its shareholders for monetary damages arising from certain breaches of the director's fiduciary duties.[110] The Model Business Nonprofit Corporation Act, which often forms the basis for state laws on this subject, includes similar provisions.

Indemnification is not a "get out of jail free card," however. Public policy dictates that a company may not indemnify directors for certain breaches. A company's indemnification generally is *not* available to a director in the case of:

- Intentional misconduct;
- Unlawful payment of dividends;
- Transactions where the director derived an improper personal benefit; or
- Insolvency of the organization or lack of resources.[111]

Individual states may require companies to provide a minimum level of indemnification for directors, then allow companies to choose whether to provide an additional permissible level of protection. When evaluating a board position, potential directors should review the company's articles of incorporation and bylaws to ensure they provide:

- Indemnification as broad as state law permits;
- *Required* rather than *permitted* indemnification for board members (This provides a greater guarantee and removes ambiguity as to when it will apply.);
- A provision that shifts the burden of proof to the company to prove that the directors and officers are not entitled to the indemnification, rather than requiring directors or officers prove that they are entitled;
- A right to appeal the company's decisions related to the scope of indemnification; and
- Advancement of defense costs, so that the expense of litigation does not drain the personal assets of a director named in a company-related lawsuit.

D&O insurance policies

Indemnification is essential to attracting and maintaining board members. The company's obligation to protect its directors and officers should not stop at indemnification, but should include an effective risk transfer mechanism such as an insurance policy.

D&O insurance has its roots in the 1930s, when Lloyds of London introduced the coverage to address personal liability exposure for directors because, at that time, corporations were not legally permitted to indemnify officers and directors.[112] In order to induce directors to sit on their boards, corporations purchased D&O coverage insurance policies on behalf of their directors and officers. As this coverage provided an additional level of comfort, D&O insurance often was referred to as "sleep insurance."[113]

Up until the 1960s, directors, officers, and their companies did not perceive a serious risk for personal liability arising from corporate activities. Consequently, D&O insurance was not prevalent. The tide turned in the 1960s, as courts began to recognize the potential personal legal liability of directors and officers; D&O insurance now is seen as an essential component of any company's risk management platform.[114] Indeed, a recent study showed that 20% of respondents said they increased their D&O limits compared to their prior policy, while only 3% said they decreased their limits.[115]

The cost of D&O insurance is cyclical, increasing, or decreasing with changes in the legal climate. In the wake of corporate scandals and significant litigation in early 2000, most companies experienced significant increases in their D&O insurance premiums. While "companies with solid finances were reporting increases in the 25% to 40% range" during 2002 and 2003, "financially precarious companies [saw] premium increases as high as 300% to 400%."[116]

Since then, insurance market pricing has stabilized. In 2004, D&O pricing actually began to decrease. Some commentators attribute this decrease to new federal laws restricting class actions, as well as to compliance provisions in SOX. As companies have increased compliance activities in the wake of these requirements, the number of securities actions filed against directors and officers has declined. Incremental D&O premium price decreases occurred from 2004 to 2010. While the class action environment has remained stable over the past few years, the pressure of the economy, impacts from new federal legislation (such as health insurance reform and Dodd-Frank), as well as new types of litigation set the stage for a possible change in trend for D&O claims.[117] According to the 2010 Towers Watson survey, the top three types of claims of greatest concern are regulatory claims, followed by direct shareholder claims and derivative claims.[118]

Personal liability risks have not been eliminated in this most recent stable market. Trends show that regulators increasingly are targeting outside directors. U.S. government scrutiny of foreign corporations and boards is increasing as well. Fifty-three percent of those responding to the 2010 Towers Watson survey stated that their companies have international operations.[119] An active merger and acquisition environment poses particular risks for directors and officers—putting at risk their personal wealth unless their company maintains adequate indemnification provisions and proper D&O coverage. Consequently, directors should inquire whether the company's D&O policy contains a level of protection commensurate with that of companies of similar size and position in similar industries.

Breaking it down—The basics of D&O coverage

D&O insurance coverage protects directors and officers against liability arising from their actions as directors and officers. Although each policy is different, and there are numerous D&O products to choose from, most policies consist of a few basic components:

- A-Side coverage,
- B-Side coverage,
- Entity coverage (or C-Side coverage),
- Employment Practices Liability (EPL) coverage,[120] and
- Sublimits for additional coverage such as HIPAA, Emergency Medical Treatment and Labor Act (EMTALA), and antitrust activities.

Prospective board members should review policy endorsements and exclusions that further expand or limit the coverage. Exclusions will differ from policy to policy, and in certain cases, exclusions can be eliminated with the payment of additional premiums.[121]

Board members also should look for D&O insurance policy enhancements that can reduce the risk of personal financial liability. This could include provisions specifying the handling of defense costs and order of payment, as well as dedicated A-Side policies.

All three of these policy elements—coverage, exclusions, and enhancements—are described below.

A-Side coverage

> ✓ Wrongful act committed by an insured *person*
> ✓ Insurance company to pay on behalf of the insured *person*

The A-Side policy provision typically covers directors and officers when either (a) the wrongful act alleged cannot be indemnified under state law or (b) the claim is indemnifiable but cannot be covered by the corporation's available financial resources. As with any insurance policy, the specific definitions of these insurance terms of art, such as "loss," "claims," and "wrongful acts" will define the scope of the coverage. Each word is important. For example, the policy's definition of wrongful act will explain exactly what kind of conduct would be deemed covered.

To ensure that a policy provides adequate protection, many advisors recommend that the policy's definition of wrongful act be as broad as possible to "include intentional and unintentional acts, errors, and omissions (including statements made) in the discharge of a director's duties, as well as any breaches of director's duties to the corporation." In addition, directors should pay careful attention to the definition of the loss, to determine if it covers everything for which the director could be held liable, including attorneys' fees, statutory damages, double and treble damages, arbitration awards, and defense costs. In most cases, insurance does not cover those penalties or other payments resulting from a director's criminal acts.[122]

While A-Side coverage is part of the standard D&O policy, additional protection can be afforded directors and officers through what is called a "dedicated A-Side policy." This type of policy may be purchased in conjunction with standard D&O coverage. Dedicated A-Side policies are discussed later in this chapter.

B-Side coverage

> ✓ Wrongful act committed by an insured *person*
> ✓ Insurance company to pay on behalf of the insured *entity*

This policy provision insures the corporation itself, in the event that the corporation is called upon to indemnify any or all of its officers and directors. This policy provision does not insure the corporation against its own liability, however.

Entity coverage (C-Side coverage)

> ✓ Wrongful act committed by an insured *entity*
> ✓ Insurance company to pay on behalf of the insured *entity*

This is the third piece of the puzzle. Entity coverage (also known as C-Side coverage) covers the corporation itself for claims made against the corporation. Claims of this nature usually are made against public corporations in connection with securities fraud. Some C-Side provisions afford coverage only when the directors and officers *and* the entity are sued. Other policies provide coverage to the company regardless of whether the directors and officers are named as defendants in the same lawsuit.

Employment Practices Liability (EPL) coverage

Policies with EPL coverage specifically cover claims relating to employment-related issues of:

- harassment, including sexual or non-sexual harassment, or creation of a hostile work environment;

- discrimination based on race, color, religion, age, sex, national origin, disability, pregnancy, medical condition, sexual orientation or preference, military status, or other status protected pursuant to federal, state, or local statute or ordinance;

- wrongful termination, demotion, or failure to promote in violation of law or against public policy;

- wage and hour, equal pay—Fair Labor Standards Act—violations;

- breach of an implied agreement to continue employment;

- retaliatory treatment against an employee; and

- employment-related misrepresentation, negligent evaluation, wrongful discipline, or wrongful deprivation of career opportunity.

As an extension of EPL coverage, some insurance companies offer coverage for third-party employment practices liability. This type of coverage insures against claims brought by third parties, such as customers or vendors, for allegations of sexual harassment or discrimination based on interactions with employees of the insured company. Typically, insurers offer this coverage at an additional premium charge.

Antitrust coverage

Many D&O policies grant sublimits of liability for other activities. For example, sublimited coverage may be provided for business-related activities such as:

- restraint of trade;

- unfair trade practices; or

- violation of the Federal Trade Commission Act, Sherman Act, Clayton Act, or other federal statutes involving Antitrust prohibitions—monopoly, price fixing, price discrimination, predatory pricing, or restraint of trade activities.

Regulatory wrongful acts by health care companies

Regulatory wrongful acts are commonly defined as acts, errors, omissions, misstatements, misconduct, fraud, reckless disregard, or negligence committed while processing bills for federal health care benefit programs. Wrongful acts also include any offer, acceptance, or payment in exchange for a patient referral, in violation of any state, local, or federal law—including Anti-kickback laws.

Crisis management services

One of the more recent additions to D&O policies is the cost of responding to crisis events, such as engaging a public relations firm to advise a company on minimizing potential harm to its reputation or financial condition from a crisis event. Examples of crisis events include the public announcement of a mass tort, a debt default, bankruptcy, loss of key executives, or a regulatory crisis.

IRS fines and penalties

Sublimited coverage also may be available to offset the assessment of taxes, initial taxes, additional taxes, tax deficiencies, excise taxes, or penalties pursuant to sections of the U.S. Internal Revenue Code.

HIPAA claims coverage

Coverage for liability arising from violations under HIPAA is generally limited to defense expenses and loss in the form of fines and penalties.

EMTALA coverage

Losses arising from violations of the Emergency Medical Treatment and Active Labor Act for health care providers may be covered in part.

Dishonesty exclusion

D&O insurance is not intended to cover claims based on deliberate or willful violations of the law, fraud, or dishonesty. (This is also true in the case of corporate indemnity of a director or officer.) Generally, these exclusions are modified by a clause stating that the knowledge of one director will not be imputed to another director for the purpose of determining whether coverage is available. This is called "severability." Further, most dishonesty exclusions have an "adjudication clause," which states that the exclusion does not apply absent an official finding of fraud or dishonesty, whether by admission, final adjudication, or judgment—including settlement.[123]

Insured vs. Insured exclusion

This provision excludes coverage when one director or officer sues either another executive of the company, as well as when the company sues its own executives. This exclusion prevents a company from orchestrating a suit against its directors and officers to collect insurance proceeds. To assure the greatest amount of protection, this exclusion should be amended so that it does not apply to:

- any cross-claim, third-party claim, or other claim for contribution or indemnity by an insured person;

- any derivative action by a security holder;

- any claim for employment practices;

- any claim by an insured person whose relationship with the company was terminated more than four years ago; or

- any claim brought on behalf of the company in bankruptcy by the company's examiner, creditor committee, trustee, receiver, liquidator, or rehabilitator, or any assignee of these particular people.

ERISA exclusion

To the extent that a company's director also acts as a fiduciary under a pension, profit sharing, or employee benefit plan maintained for that company, the D&O policy will not insure for any liability under ERISA. ERISA can be a source of personal liability for these directors, so they should consider seeking separate fiduciary liability coverage.

Prior Acts exclusion

This provision bars insurance coverage for wrongful acts that occurred prior to a specified time period—usually coinciding with termination of coverage under a previous policy or change in control of the corporation. Where this is a concern, most corporations will purchase "tail" coverage to cover any claims that were covered under the old policy but will not be under the new policy.

Professional Liability exclusion

This provision bars coverage for liability associated with professional services. For example, if a doctor is the president of a professional corporation, the D&O coverage would not insure the doctor for malpractice claims. This distinction seems obvious. In practice, however, the distinction between acts performed in a professional capacity and those within the purview of a corporation's officers and directors may be subtle. In the health care industry, professional liability exclusions commonly disallow exposures such as medical malpractice and managed care errors and omissions. Prospective board members should consider whether they have purchased adequate coverage for those exposures separately.

Bodily Injury, Property Damage, Environmental exclusions

This provision bars bodily injury and property damage claims. For example, an executive's insurance might cover a shareholder claim relating to environmental compliance issues, but exclude claims brought by property owners or regulators for damages resulting from the underlying environmental claim.

Defense costs

Most D&O policies cover defense costs and liabilities. Policies differ, however, on which circumstances require the insurer to cover defense costs and when these defense costs must be paid. For example, some policies specify whether the costs should be advanced as they are incurred, or whether they should be reimbursed at the end of the process.

D&O insurers have a strong financial interest in making certain that insured directors and officers are vigorously and well defended. This suggests that the insurer would want to be involved in management of the claim. In certain circumstances, however, such as where intentional misconduct is alleged, the case ultimately may constitute an excluded claim not covered by the D&O policy. In these circumstances, early involvement of the insurer may not be warranted. The dilemma for the insurer is that it may be difficult or impossible to determine whether the claim is excluded from coverage until the ultimate resolution of the case. As a solution, most policies require the insurer to advance the costs of the defense at the outset and during the case. If the case is excluded from coverage in the end, the director or the company may be required to reimburse the insurer.[124]

Defense costs can be quite expensive. As described earlier, directors face the risk of being sued. Prospective board members should ensure that the company's D&O policy expressly requires the insurer to advance defense costs. The company also may want to avoid any requirement for any security or collateral delivered to the insurer in return for advancing defense costs.

Punitive damages

Although most policies exclude fines and penalties from loss, policies deal with punitive damages in a variety of ways. Policies may cover punitive damages, exclude them along with fines and penalties, or expressly state that punitive damages are not part of a "loss."

Not all states permit insurers to cover punitive damages. State law may allow full insurance coverage, prohibit coverage, or authorize coverage for vicarious liability only. To avail themselves of the broadest interpretation available, prospective board members should request the enhancement of "Most

Favorable Venue." This insurance contract provision requires the insurer to evaluate the state or location when determining the extent to which punitive damages are insurable, thus expanding the potential for coverage of punitive damages.

Order of Payment

Historically, D&O policies protected the directors and officers of a company. As the D&O policy has evolved in market segments such as health care, it has come to cover a broader range of entities—the organization, trustees, committee members, managers, volunteers, and employees. As settlements rise and litigation continues to occur, competition for the limits of the D&O policy intensifies. Directors and officers might find themselves without the coverage they need to protect their personal assets if numerous parties are named in a suit, the policy limits are insufficient to satisfy the settlement, and indemnification is not available.

The "Order of Payment" clause protects directors and officers and assures them that the company's obligation to indemnify the directors is a recognized priority. This clause, where legally permissible, provides that the personal protection of A-Side coverage shall have priority over claims under the entity protection of B-Side and C-Side coverage.

Dedicated A-Side policy

This type of D&O policy provides directors and officers with personal asset protection when indemnification and insurance are not available or when the limits of the underlying policies are exhausted. As described above, there often are numerous parties competing for recovery under the same D&O policy. Directors and officers can add an additional line of defense dedicated solely to them through the purchase of a dedicated A-Side D&O policy. This coverage is purely for the directors and officers of the company. It does not provide any coverage for the company, nor does it provide coverage to other insured persons who may be covered in the primary policy.

Dedicated A-Side coverage typically is purchased as a top layer excess limit that sits above all the D&O coverage limits. Dedicated A-Side limits are in addition to the traditional

D&O policy A-Side limits, or in the event that the B-side or C-side entity coverage limits are exhausted. The dedicated A-Side policy would respond with dedicated coverage available only for the directors and officers. Another benefit of the dedicated A-Side policy is that its limits are protected from being frozen or seized as an asset of the company in bankruptcy proceedings, because the company is not an insured—this D&O policy is not considered a corporate asset.

In addition, an enhancement to the dedicated A-Side policy may increase its value and the commensurate protection it offers the directors and officers. A feature called the "DIC (difference in coverage) drop down" extends broader coverage for non-indemnifiable loss. The DIC drop down has fewer exclusions and often is non-rescindable by the insurance company. This A-Side DIC policy preserves coverage when:

- the primary policy does not respond,

- the organization cannot indemnify,

- the organization denies indemnification,

- underlying limits have been exhausted, or

- broader terms have been negotiated for the directors and officers.

Purchasing D&O insurance policies

Board members should consider seeking expert advice when preparing a D&O insurance application. The law in some states supports D&O insurance company denial of coverage when there has been a material misrepresentation of facts in the application. Beyond that, directors are well advised to ask questions of the auditors, management, CFO, employees, and outside experts when the company presents information about D&O insurance policies. Additionally, many professional associations provide members with guidance and benchmarking about insurance purchasing and coverage.

Questions to be asked include:

- Who is the insurance broker? Does the broker understand the company's business? Is the broker experienced in placing D&O insurance? How many insurance companies does the broker have direct access to?

- What insurance companies offer D&O policies? How often are carriers asked to compete for the company's policy? This is important to ensure that the best coverage is purchased at the best price.

- Why was one insurance company chosen rather than another? The decision should not be limited to price. Familiarize yourself with the insurance company.
  - What is the financial strength of the insurance company—what is its rating from the various rating agencies?
  - Has the current insurance company been a reliable partner? Has the company kept its promises?
  - How long has the insurance company been in the D&O insurance marketplace? What is the insurance company's management, underwriting, and claims experience?
  - Is the insurance company committed to the D&O insurance product?

- What are the D&O policy terms and conditions? Ask that they be listed and explained to your satisfaction.
  - Are the D&O policy limits adequate? Ask for benchmarking of coverage and premiums with similar companies.
  - It there a policy retention, deductible, or coinsurance? If so, who is responsible for paying it?
  - Are there any exclusions to the D&O policy? If so, why?
  - Are there any sublimits, sub-retentions or coinsurance in the D&O policy for certain types of exposures such as EPL, Antitrust, punitive damages, or class actions?
  - What coverages are afforded under the policy for regulatory wrongful act claims? Does the definition of claim include the investigation costs?
  - Is EPL coverage afforded under the policy? If not, is there a separate policy?

- How does the insurance company manage claims? What is its position on denying, settling, or vigorously defending claims?

  • What can you expect after reporting a claim?

  • Is there a predetermined panel of defense counsel? If so, are they experienced in defending claims against directors and officers?

  • What are the insurance company's claim reporting requirements? How does it reserve claims?

- Does the carrier offer risk management assistance? Look for value added services such as board of directors' liability educational resources and programs. Insurance companies also may provide invaluable assistance with employment practices risk management information, training, and legal hotline services that can be accessed for legal advice when a problem occurs.

Information and review of the D&O insurance policies should be part of a board's annual education. Inquire every year about any changes in insurance company, D&O policy limits, or coverage. Stay informed on all claims or potential claims under the D&O policy. The insurance broker also should provide industry information through written materials as well as live consultations.

Conclusion

Given how essential adequate D&O coverage can be for a director in this era of regulatory change, such as health care reform and increased scrutiny of corporate governance, a director should seek expert advice in reviewing his or her D&O policy (not just the proposal from the broker, but the actual, seemingly impenetrable language of the policy itself). Whenever a company is about to embark upon a fundamental transaction such as a merger, initial public offering, or joint venture, an expert can be instrumental in ensuring that the D&O policy is amended and expanded to an appropriate level to maintain the protection needed for the company's directors and officers. D&O policy coverage is an area where prospective and current directors need to be proactive.

5 How Does the Sarbanes-Oxley Act Impact Directors and Boardroom Practices?

On July 30, 2002, President George W. Bush signed into law The Public Company Accounting Reform and Investor Protection Act, better known as the Sarbanes-Oxley Act of 2002.[125] SOX mandated one of the most far-reaching changes Congress has imposed on the public company business world since FDR's New Deal. SOX was and is an effort to prevent scandal and restore investor confidence in publicly traded companies.

Eight years later, the benefits of a law that some called the "corporate equivalent of a root canal"[126] are still debated. Many CEOs acknowledge some of the benefits of improved internal controls, increased investor confidence, and increased transparency. At the same time, companies continue to struggle to adjust to the increased fees and complexity of performing audits, and to the many new costs associated with greater internal controls.[127]

An amendment to the Securities and Exchange Act of 1934, SOX only applies to public companies that issue stock and list their securities on a national securities exchange, such as the NYSE or NASDAQ. However, SOX has inspired similar rulemaking reforms for Self-Regulatory Organizations (SROs) such as the NYSE, NASDAQ, and non-profit organizations.

Many in the business world saw SOX as a set of new corporate governance best practices for all companies and their boards of directors. Whether a company's stock is publicly traded or privately held, and whether the company is for profit or non-profit, company leaders should consider the benefits of adopting the SOX standards of governance. Even in the non-profit environment, the rating agencies have adopted similar SOX-type provisions as non-profit best practices.

SOX 101: Key provisions

SOX is organized into eleven sections, called "titles." Prospective board members should be familiar with the requirements set forth in the titles that deal with:

1. accounting oversight,

2. auditor independence,

3. corporate accountability,

4. financial disclosures,

5. conflicts of interest,

6. fraud accountability and white collar crime penalties, and

7. whistleblower protections.

The following sections briefly describe the requirements in each of these titles.

Accounting oversight

SOX established an oversight board called the Public Company Accounting Oversight Board (PCAOB).[128] The PCAOB oversees audits of public companies. Any accounting firm performing an audit of a public company must register with the PCAOB. The PCAOB recently was challenged in a Supreme Court case addressing the way that the PCAOB removes members of its board. In the past, PCAOB members were appointed by the SEC, but could only be removed by the SEC for cause—creating a substantial tenure of many PCAOB members. On June 28, 2010, the Supreme Court ruled that the manner in which the members of the PCAOB could be removed was unconstitutional as a violation of the separation of powers. The SEC can now remove PCAOB members at will.[129]

When the opinion was released, headlines around the United States speculated that striking down a portion of SOX would have a significant impact on public companies and that the PCAOB would cease to exist. However, companies with registration requirements and other involvement with the PCAOB are unlikely to see much impact. In its opinion, the Supreme Court made clear that only the specific PCAOB member removal restrictions were invalid. Otherwise "[t]he Sarbanes-Oxley Act remains 'fully operative as a law'. . . ." [130]

Even in the non-profit sector, the PCAOB and its rules affect companies because audit firms subjected to these rules do not, as a general matter, differentiate their services.

Auditor independence

The indictment of a major accounting firm provided the main impetus for audit reforms. SOX aimed to eliminate conflicts of interest in audits. SOX limits what other services an accounting firm may provide to companies when the accounting firm is that company's independent auditor. SOX also mandates periodic rotation of audit partners on each account.

> See Chapter Six for an in-depth discussion of the various standards for auditor independence, and Chapter Seven for a description of the SEC's final rules on composition and responsibility of audit committees.

Corporate accountability

SOX increases the accountability of directors, officers, and corporate legal counsel. SOX required the SEC to enact rules on reporting by attorneys employed by a corporation. Attorneys, both in-house and outside, are required to report internally evidence of a material violation of a securities law, a breach of fiduciary duty, or similar violation by the company to the chief legal counsel or CEO. If the chief legal counsel or the CEO does not respond appropriately, the attorney must report the incident to a committee of the board of directors comprised exclusively of outside directors. [131]

SOX requires that each annual or quarterly report filed with the SEC be accompanied by a certification by the chief executive officer *and* the chief financial officer. These certifications must include assurances of compliance with securities laws, as well as statements that the reports fairly present, in all material respects, the financial condition and operational results of the company.[132] Violators of these rules may be penalized with forfeiture of compensation for one year following any misstatement. A board member who also serves in the role of CEO should consider these requirements and the significant implications of false certifications carefully.

Financial disclosures

SOX requires public companies to disclose in plain English—and on a rapid and current basis—information concerning material changes in their financial condition or operations. SOX shortened the filing deadline for Section 16 reports, which disclose changes in beneficial ownership, to two days.[133] Also, SOX requires the SEC to review public company disclosures at least once every three years.

How does the SEC schedule these reviews? A company's name might surface on the list for review if the company:

- has issued material restatements of financial results,

- has experienced significant volatility in stock price as compared with other public companies,

- has a large market share (i.e., how big is the company?),

- is a new company with disparities in its price to earnings ratios (i.e., the stock price is unusual given company profits), or if

- company operations significantly affect any major sector of the economy.

Conflict of interest

SOX requires a public company to disclose whether it has adopted a code of ethics applicable to its principal financial officer and principal accounting officer.[134] If there is no such code of ethics, the company must explain why.[135]

Fraud accountability and white collar crime penalties

SOX extended the statute of limitations for securities fraud to the earlier of (1) two years after the discovery of facts constituting the violation or (2) five years after the violation. SOX also extended the maximum prison term for securities fraud to twenty-five years and imposed criminal penalties for the knowing destruction, alteration, and falsification of documents in federal investigations and bankruptcy proceedings.

Among the penalties: Any officer who signs an SEC certification knowing that the report is not correct may be fined up to $1 million and/or imprisoned for up to ten years. A willful violation is punishable by a fine of up to $5 million and/or imprisonment for up to twenty years.

Whistleblower protection

A whistleblower is an individual who lawfully provides information or assists in an investigation relating to a violation of federal securities law or securities fraud.[136] SOX provides that no company, or any of its officers, employees or contractors, may discharge, demote, suspend, threaten, harass, or discriminate against a whistleblower in any other manner.

The Dodd-Frank Act, mentioned earlier in this book, added rewards and protections for whistleblowers. On the rewards side, the Dodd-Frank Act "creates a program within the SEC to encourage people to report securities violations, creating rewards of up to 30% of funds recovered for information provided."[137] Prior to the Dodd-Frank Act, the SEC reward structure allowed the whistleblower to receive 10% of funds recovered, and only in insider trading cases.[138] Additional protections allow the whistleblower to sue in federal court any employer who retaliates. (In the past, there were a number of administrative steps the whistleblower would have needed to take before suing the employer.)

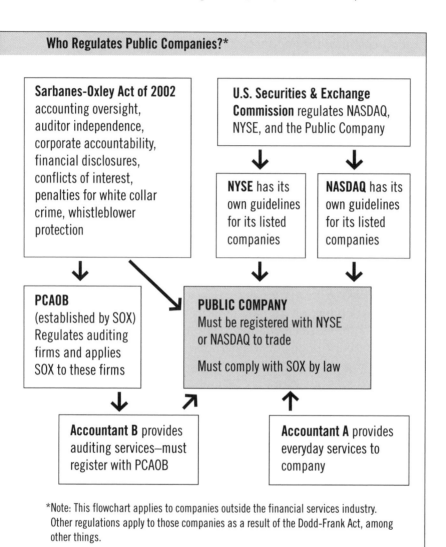

Who Regulates Public Companies?*

Sarbanes-Oxley Act of 2002 accounting oversight, auditor independence, corporate accountability, financial disclosures, conflicts of interest, penalties for white collar crime, whistleblower protection

U.S. Securities & Exchange Commission regulates NASDAQ, NYSE, and the Public Company

NYSE has its own guidelines for its listed companies

NASDAQ has its own guidelines for its listed companies

PCAOB (established by SOX) Regulates auditing firms and applies SOX to these firms

PUBLIC COMPANY Must be registered with NYSE or NASDAQ to trade

Must comply with SOX by law

Accountant B provides auditing services—must register with PCAOB

Accountant A provides everyday services to company

*Note: This flowchart applies to companies outside the financial services industry. Other regulations apply to those companies as a result of the Dodd-Frank Act, among other things.

Advanced SOX: Issues for directors

With that backdrop, the question remains: Which provisions of SOX should directors concern themselves with most? Although several provisions of SOX implicate directors' behavior and corporate governance in general, a few specific areas are of particular concern.

Be prepared for Section 404: Internal controls over financial reporting

Section 404 of SOX focuses on the efficiency of a public company's internal control over financial reporting. While many have criticized Section 404 openly, others believe that increased spending on internal controls actually will save money by pushing management to streamline operations. Collaboration among different departments and cooperation with accountants not only will enhance corporate compliance and internal controls, but also may cut costs by preventing duplicate work product and improving interdepartmental communications.

To whom does SOX apply?

Like most of SOX, Section 404 reports are mandatory only for public companies listed on a national exchange. There is a trend towards voluntary application to private and non-profit companies, however.[139] In the spring of 2005, a GAO report found that Section 404 costs are disproportionately high for small companies, causing some to abandon the public equity markets and go private.[140]

In response to these concerns, the SEC announced plans to revisit some of the SOX rules, including Rule 404. On May 23, 2007, the SEC approved new guidance to help these smaller companies "strengthen their internal control over financial reporting while reducing unnecessary costs."[141] Beginning with their 2007 annual reports, smaller companies began complying with Section 404. However, in the Dodd-Frank Act passed in July 2010 (discussed more fully in Chapter Three), small public companies (with a market value of less than $75 million) were granted an exemption from the internal control audit requirements of Section 404.[142] The exemption aims to reduce the burden of 404 compliance for smaller companies.[143]

Pay attention to situations involving loans to officers and directors

Board members, especially those on the compensation committee, may want to pay particular attention to the developing law around SOX rules related to loans to officers and seek guidance from advisors. This provision of SOX could affect cashless exercise of stock options, travel advances, and even advancement of D&O expenses and defense costs—transactions previously considered ordinary.

Be prepared to disclose company information fast

SOX requires practically a nonstop stream of information from the company to the general public.[144] What disclosures are necessary?

- Form 10-Q (a quarterly report of financial position),
- Form 10-K (a yearly report of financial position), and
- Form 8-K (a report of unscheduled events or company changes, typically filed four days after a triggering event).

Previously, Form 8K filings only included events such as bankruptcy, acquisition, director changes, or similar material events. Now, companies must file Form 8K when other events occur, including entry into or termination of unusual material agreements, or the creation of a financial obligation that will not appear on the balance sheet.[145] Additionally, SOX allows companies to use Form 8K to comply with "Regulation FD"—the fair disclosure regulation. This regulation requires companies to notify the public when the company discovers a leak of non-public information.

SOX shortened the time frames for all of these filings. In response to these rules, a board, and, in particular, the committees of the board, should begin to prepare for the time when companies will be expected to disclose much more information about financial and business changes than in the past, and much more quickly. Board members may want to ask management about the procedures and controls needed to comply with these rules.

Treat whistleblowers with caution

SOX addresses the issue of whistleblowers as follows:

(1) Companies can be delisted from national securities exchanges if they do not have procedures to receive and appropriately address employee whistleblower complaints about company accounting practices. The audit committee must oversee and closely supervise these procedures. You may be familiar with anonymous hotlines or website services that receive whistleblower complaints. These methods may be expanded, as a result of SOX, to include complaints relating to specific accounting issues.

(2) Whistleblowers can file a civil suit if they believe they were wrongfully discharged, harassed, or discriminated against because of their whistleblower actions.

(3) SOX makes it a felony to take harmful action against a whistleblower.[146]

Understand the role of the company's lawyers

Board members should become familiar with inside and outside counsel's role with respect to the corporation and the directors. These lawyers represent the company as a legal entity—not individual directors. On many issues, the interests of the individual board members and the company are aligned; the company's lawyers, in effect, may represent the interests of the board. In other situations, however, board members may need to seek their own separate counsel to ensure that their personal interests are being served.

Lawyers are expected to report breaches and violations "up the ladder," reporting incidents to the CEO, chief legal officer, or the audit committee as necessary.

The SEC requires companies to establish a qualified legal compliance committee (QLCC). To qualify as a QLCC, a committee must include at least one member of the company's audit committee and two or more independent board members. A QLCC must adopt written procedures for receiving and resolving reports of material noncompliance.[147]

What are the immediate and long term effects of SOX?

SOX undoubtedly has had a major impact on the operations of public boards of directors. It has begun to influence the governance practices of private company boards and non-profits' boards of trustees as well. Immediately following its enactment, SOX set off a wave of state legislative proposals that mimicked SOX on the state level.[148] While it currently appears that states will not adopt SOX-like regulations for private companies, those companies widely recognize the benefits of structuring and implementing a SOX-like compliance program.

Any conscientious director on the board of a public company should be intimately familiar with the ever-evolving SOX rules and regulations. A director on the board of any company (public or private) should keep generally informed about SOX's overall corporate governance implications. All directors should ensure that they are kept apprised of applicable state law initiatives relating to corporate governance and reporting requirements. Finally, directors should note that not all provisions of SOX became effective upon enactment in 2002. Directors should keep up to date with the interpretive rules that the SEC periodically issues.

As described in this chapter, SOX established new legal requirements. Even where those requirements do not apply, SOX has ushered in a trend towards stricter scrutiny and enforcement. Whether sitting on the board of a public, private, or non-profit company, a director always should follow the basic tenets surrounding a director's fiduciary duties—the duty of care and the duty of loyalty.

6 How Do the NYSE and NASDAQ Listing Standards Shape Board Requirements?

WITH CONTRIBUTIONS BY
Lola Miranda Hale, Epstein Becker & Green, P.C.

History of the NYSE and NASDAQ

Before the New York Stock Exchange was established, stockbrokers and other merchants bought and sold most securities in and around the coffee houses and office buildings in the Wall Street area of Manhattan. Persons wishing to conduct a securities transaction had to search out a willing buyer or seller; there were no set times or places for these transactions.[149]

The NYSE traces its origins to May 17, 1792 when 24 stockbrokers signed an agreement to trade with one another beneath a Buttonwood Tree outside 68 Wall Street.[150] Today, the NYSE, which recently converted to a for profit corporation called the NYSE Group,[151] is a thriving exchange listing approximately 2,700 companies.[152] On February 9, 2011, it was reported that, after 219 years, the NYSE was near agreement to be acquired by Deutsche Börse in a transaction that would create the world's largest financial stock exchange.[153]

In contrast, NASDAQ began trading on February 8, 1971, heralding itself as the world's first electronic stock market.[154] Unlike a floor-based exchange, NASDAQ's market makers and trading systems connect into NASDAQ from all across the globe. Currently, NASDAQ lists more companies and conducts more trades per day than any other U.S. market, with 3,200 listed companies.[155]

Sarbanes Oxley Act and the NYSE and NASDAQ listing standards

In November 2003, the Securities and Exchange Commission approved proposed amendments to the NYSE and NASDAQ corporate governance listing standards. These standards were proposed in response to SOX mandates.

Given that most U.S. public companies are listed on either the NYSE or the NASDAQ, when these exchanges proposed new and stricter listing standards, the landscape of corporate governance for the majority of the business community was substantially changed.[156] Companies listed on these exchanges immediately sought education on the new listing standards, modifying, as appropriate, compliance procedures and the composition of boards and committees—and searching for independent directors. Many of these companies had spent the previous year working to comply with SOX, but the new listing standards required them to implement additional compliance measures.

The most revolutionary of the changes were the new "independence" requirements for the composition of the board and its committees. The independence requirements mandated that boards, for the first time, reach outside their immediate contacts to find suitable "independent" director candidates. As one of the SEC Commissioners stated in a 2005 speech:

> *[The independence requirements] alone immediately opened seats in the [b]oardroom [and] ... entry into the boardroom is no longer controlled by the old saying of "it's not what you know, but who you know" ... there is no question that it's now what you know that matters.*[157]

Dodd Frank Act

The Dodd-Frank Act of 2010 continues the themes in SOX with additional corporate governance, executive compensation disclosure, and other provisions that apply to public companies listed on exchanges. In particular, the Dodd-Frank Act requires the SEC to promulgate rules requiring stock exchanges to adopt, as additional listing standards, requirements for an independent compensation committee of the board of directors. The definition of independence is similar to the definition for independent audit committee members under SOX. Thus, companies wishing to be listed on (or continue to be listed on) a securities exchange will be required to have independent directors who can serve on the compensation committee.

The listing standards: A summary and comparison

As mentioned above, the NYSE and NASDAQ exchanges had already adopted corporate governance listing standards on the heels of SOX—including an independence mandate for a majority of the board of directors. The exchanges have provided several tests for determining the independence of directors under their respective—similar but not identical—listing standards.[158]

The charts below compare the exchanges' independence and other corporate governance standards in effect prior to implementation of Dodd-Frank. References to "company" include parent and subsidiaries in a consolidated group with the listed company or other company relevant to a determination under the independence standards.[159]

General Independence Requirement	
NYSE[160]	**NASDAQ**[161]
A majority of the board must be independent.	A majority of the board must be independent.
Board Determination of Independence	
NYSE	**NASDAQ**
The board must affirmatively determine that the director has no material relationship with the company (either directly as a partner, shareholder, or officer of any organization that has a relationship with the company).	The board has a responsibility, through the application of Rule 5605(a)(2), to make an affirmative determination that directors do not have a relationship with the company that would impair their independence. Rule 5605(a)(2) also provides a list of certain relationships that preclude a board finding of independence.

Bright-Line Independence Tests *	
NYSE	**NASDAQ**
The following persons would **not** be considered independent for a particular company: ■ An individual, who is or was an employee of the company within the last 3 years, or whose immediate family has been an executive officer within the last 3 years; ■ An individual who received, or whose immediate family has received, during any 12 month period within the last 3 years more than $120,000 in direct compensation from the company (other than director and committee fees or deferred compensation for prior service, provided it is not contingent on continued service); ■ The director is a current employee, or an immediate family member is a current executive officer, of another company that has made payments to, or received payments from, the company for property or services in an amount which, in any of the last 3 fiscal years, exceeds the greater of $1 million, or 2% of such other company's consolidated gross revenues; ■ The director or an immediate family member is, or has been with the last 3 years, employed as an	The following persons would **not** be considered independent for a particular company: ■ An individual who is or was within the last 3 years, employed by the company or any subsidiary of the company; ■ A director who is a family member of an individual who is or was employed as an executive officer by the company or any affiliate of the company during the past 3 years; ■ A director who accepted, or who has a family member who accepted, any compensation from the company in excess of $120,000 during any period of 12 consecutive months within the 3 years preceding the determination of independence (other than compensation for board or board committee service, compensation paid to a family member who is an employee (other than an executive officer) of the company, or benefits under a tax-qualified retirement plan, or non-discretionary compensation); ■ A director who is, or has a family member who is, a partner, a controlling shareholder, or an *continues*

---

* A bright-line test is defined as "a clearly defined rule or standard, generally used in law, composed of objective factors, which leaves little or no room for varying interpretation."

Bright-Line Independence Tests *continued*	
NYSE	**NASDAQ**
executive officer of another company where any of the company's present executive officers at the same time serves or served on that company's compensation committee; ▪ The director is a current partner or employee of a firm that is the company's internal or external auditor; ▪ The director has an immediate family member who is a current partner of such a firm; ▪ The director has an immediate family member who is a current employee of such a firm and personally works on the listed company's audit; or ▪ The director or an immediate family member was within the last 3 years a partner or employee of such a firm and personally worked on the listed company's audit within that time.	executive officer in any organization to which the company made or from which the company received payments for property or services in the current or any of the last 3 years that exceed 5% of the recipient's consolidated gross revenues for that year or $200,000, whichever is more (except for certain exempted transactions), other than payments arising solely from investments in the company's securities or payments under non-discretionary charitable contribution matching programs; ▪ A director who is, or has a family member who is, employed as an executive officer of another entity where at any time during the past 3 years the executive officers of the company have served on such other company's compensation committee; or ▪ A director who is, or has a family member who is, a current partner of the company's outside auditor or was a partner or employee of the company's outside auditor who worked on the company's audit at any time during the past 3 years.

Other Corporate Governance Standards

Disclosure Requirements

NYSE[162]	NASDAQ[163]
Each company must disclose in its annual proxy statement (or if it does not file an annual proxy statement in its annual report on Form 10-K) that its corporate governance guidelines and its code of business conduct and ethics are each available on its website and provide the address.	The company must disclose in its annual proxy (or, if the company does not file a proxy, in its Form 10-K or 20-F) those directors that the board of directors has determined to be independent under Rule 5605(a)(2).
Each company CEO must notify the NYSE promptly after any executive officer becomes aware of "any" noncompliance with the NYSE governance standards.	Each company must provide NASDAQ with prompt notification after an executive officer of the company becomes aware of any noncompliance by the company with the requirements of the Rule 5600 Series.
The nomination/corporate governance, compensation, and audit committees' charters must be available on the company website, with availability and the website address disclosed in the annual proxy statement—or if not filed, on its Form 10-K.	Any waivers of the code of ethics for directors or executive officers must be approved by the board. Companies, other than Foreign Private Issuers, must disclose such waivers within 4 business days by filing a current report on Form 8-K with the Commission or, in cases where a Form 8-K is not required, by distributing a press release.
Each company must comply with the disclosure requirements of Item 407 of Regulation S-K regarding the identity of directors meeting the applicable independence standards.	
The following must be disclosed by the company either on its website or in its annual proxy statement—or, if does not file an annual proxy	

continues

Other Corporate Governance Standards *continued*	
Disclosure Requirements	
NYSE	**NASDAQ**
statement, in its annual report on Form 10-K: (a) if within the preceding 3 years company contributions to tax exempt organization in which any independent director serves as an executive officer exceeded the greater of $1 million or 2% of such organization's consolidated gross revenues; (b) if 1 director presides at all executive sessions, his or her name must be disclosed; (c) the method for persons to communicate directly with the presiding director or with independent or non-management directors as a group; and (d) the determination made regarding the effectiveness of an audit committee member who serves on more than 3 public company audit committees. If disclosure is made on or through the website, the company must disclose that fact in its annual proxy statement or annual report, as applicable, and provide the website address.	

Other Corporate Governance Standards	
Annual Certifications	
NYSE[162]	**NASDAQ**[163]
Each company CEO must certify annually that he or she is not aware of any violation by the company of any NYSE corporate governance listing standards.	Each company must promptly notify NASDAQ after any executive officer becomes aware of any material noncompliance with the corporate governance standards, but there is no specific annual certification requirement.
Audit Committees	
NYSE	**NASDAQ**
Each company must have an audit committee that satisfies Rule 10A-3 of the Securities and Exchange Act of 1934, as amended (requiring, among other things, that the audit committee be composed entirely of independent directors).	Each company must have an "all-independent" audit committee of at least 3 members, who meet the criteria for independence of Rule 10A-3, have not participated in the preparation of the company's or any current subsidiary's financial statements at any time during the last 3 years, and who have the ability to read and understand fundamental financial statements.
The audit committee must have at least 3 members, each financially literate.	
At least 1 member must have accounting and related financial management expertise as the board interprets such qualification in its business judgment. Although a financial expert, as defined in Item 407(d)(5)(ii) of Regulation S-K, is not required by the NYSE, the board may presume that the expert has accounting or related financial management expertise.	In addition to satisfying the Independent Director requirements, audit committee members must meet the criteria for independence set forth in Rule 10A-3(b)(1) under the Exchange Act. They must not accept any consulting, advisory, or other compensatory fee from the company other than for board service, and they must not be an affiliated person of the company.
In addition, to meeting the NYSE's director independence standards,	*continues*

Other Corporate Governance Standards

Audit Committees *continued*

NYSE	NASDAQ
an audit committee member must meet the criteria for independence set forth in Rule 10A-3(b)(1) and as such cannot, subject to certain limited exceptions: (i) accept, directly or indirectly, any consulting, advisory, or other compensatory fee (other than board or committee fees) from the listed company or any subsidiary, or (ii) be an affiliated person of the company or any subsidiary. If an audit committee member serves on more than 3 public company audit committees, the board must determine that such service would not impair the ability of the member to serve effectively. This determination must be disclosed on its website or in its annual proxy statement or 10-K. Each company must have an internal audit function to provide management and the audit committee with ongoing assessments of risk management processes and systems of internal control. The audit committee must have a written charter. (The standards detail specific minimum information that charter must include.)	Audit committees must have at least 1 financial expert—a person with past employment experience in finance or accounting, requisite professional certification in accounting, or any other comparable experience or background that results in the individual's financial sophistication, including being or having been a chief executive officer, chief financial officer, or other senior officer with financial oversight responsibilities. Each company must certify that it has adopted a formal written audit committee charter and that the audit committee has reviewed and reassessed the adequacy annually. (The standards detail specific minimum information that the charter must include.)

Other Corporate Governance Standards	
Code of Conduct and Governance Guidelines	
NYSE	**NASDAQ**
Each company must adopt and disclose a code of business conduct and ethics for directors, officers, and employees and promptly disclose any waivers of the code for directors or executive officers. The code should address conflicts, corporate opportunity, confidentiality, fair dealing, protection and proper use of company assets, compliance with laws, rules, and regulations (including insider trading laws), and must encourage reporting of illegal or unethical behavior. Each company must adopt and disclose corporate governance guidelines, and these guidelines must be posted on the company's website. The guidelines should address topics such as director qualification standards, director responsibilities, director access to management, director compensation, director orientation and continuing education, management succession, and annual performance evaluations of the board.	Each company must adopt a code of conduct applicable to all directors, officers, and employees, and must make the code publicly available. The code of conduct must require that any waiver of the code for executive officers or directors be made only by the board and be promptly disclosed to shareholders. A code of conduct satisfying this rule must comply with the definition of a "code of ethics" set out in Section 406(c) of SOX. The code must provide for an enforcement mechanism.
Shareholder Approval of Share Issuances and Equity Plans	
NYSE	**NASDAQ**
With limited exceptions noted in the standards, shareholders must be	Shareholder approval is required prior to an issuance of securities in

continues

Other Corporate Governance Standards

Shareholder Approval of Share Issuances and Equity Plans *continued*

NYSE	NASDAQ
given an opportunity to vote on all equity compensation plans and material revisions. (Shareholder approval provisions for stock issuances are addressed in the rules but are not addressed in the corporate governance section of the rules.)	connection with: (i) the acquisition of the stock or assets of another company; (ii) equity-based compensation of officers, directors, employees, or consultants; (iii) a change of control; and (iv) certain private placements.

Voting Rights

NYSE	NASDAQ
Voting rights of existing shareholders of publicly traded common stock registered under Section 12 of the Exchange Act cannot be disparately reduced or restricted through any corporate action or issuance. (These rules are not contained within the corporate governance rules of the NYSE.)	A company cannot create a new class of security that votes at a higher rate than an existing class of securities, or take any other action that has the effect of restricting or reducing the voting rights of an existing class of securities.

Annual Shareholder Meetings

NYSE	NASDAQ
Companies are required to hold an annual meeting each fiscal year.	Companies (other than limited partnerships that meet certain requirements) are required to hold an annual meeting of shareholders no later than 1 year after the end of the company's fiscal year-end.

Other Corporate Governance Standards	

Related Party Transactions Oversight	
NYSE	**NASDAQ**
No similarly specific requirement.	Each company that is not a limited partnership must conduct an appropriate review and oversight of all related party transactions for potential conflict of interest situations on an ongoing basis by the company's audit committee or another independent body of the board of directors.

Date of Standards' First Effectiveness	
NYSE	**NASDAQ**
Companies listing on the NYSE are required to comply with all applicable requirements of Section 303A as of date that the company's securities first trade on the NYSE (the "listing date") with certain exceptions for certain types of companies. A company listing in conjunction with its IPO is required to comply as follows: • The company must satisfy the majority independent board requirement of Section 303A.01, if applicable, within 1 year of the listing date. • The company must satisfy the website posting requirements of corporate governance rules by the earlier of the date the IPO closes or 5 business days from the listing date.	The rules provide a phase-in schedule for nominating and compensation committee requirements for a company listing in connection with its IPO, and for certain types of companies. A company listing in conjunction with its IPO must have: (a) 1 independent member at the time of listing, (b) a majority of independent members within 90 days of listing, and (c) all independent members within 1 year of listing. A company listing in connection with its IPO has 12 months from the date of listing to comply with *continues*

Other Corporate Governance Standards	
Date of Standards' First Effectiveness *continued*	
NYSE	**NASDAQ**
• The company must have at least: (a) 1 independent member on its nominating committee and at least 1 independent member on its compensation committee, by the earlier of the date the IPO closes or 5 business days from the listing date, (b) at least a majority of independent members on each committee within 90 days of the listing date, and (c) fully independent committees within 1 year of the listing date. • The company must have at least: (a) 1 independent member on its audit committee that satisfies the requirements of Rule 10A-3 and Section 303A.02 by the listing date, (b) at least a majority of independent members on its audit committee within 90 days of the effective date of its registration statement, and (c) a fully independent audit committee within 1 year of the effective date of its registration statement.	the majority independent board requirement in Rule 5605(b). Companies may choose not to adopt a compensation or nomination committee and may instead rely upon a majority of the Independent Directors to discharge responsibilities under Rule 5605(b).

Other Corporate Governance Standards

Executive Sessions

NYSE	NASDAQ
The non-management directors must meet at regularly scheduled executive sessions without management.	The independent directors must have regularly scheduled meetings at which only independent directors are present.

Internal Audit Function

NYSE	NASDAQ
Each company must have an internal audit function to provide management and the audit committee with ongoing assessments of the company's risk management processes and internal controls.	No similarly specific requirement.

Nominating and Compensation Committees

NYSE	NASDAQ
Companies must have a nominating/corporate governance committee and a separate compensation committee, each composed entirely of independent directors.	Not required as separate committees. The company may instead rely upon a majority of the independent directors to discharge responsibilities under the rules.
The nominating/corporate governance committee and the compensation committee must each have a written charter. (The standards detail specific minimum information that each charter must include.)	Nominees for director must be selected by a majority of the independent directors or an "all-independent" nominating committee.
Section 952 of the Dodd-Frank Act added a new Section 10C to the Exchange Act requiring the SEC to direct the national securities exchanges and associations to	A formal written charter or resolution addressing the director nomination process must be adopted.
	Compensation of the CEO and all other executive officers must be

continues

Other Corporate Governance Standards	
Nominating and Compensation Committees *continued*	
NYSE	**NASDAQ**
prohibit the listing of any equity security of a company unless all compensation committee members are independent and meet enhanced independence requirements.	determined by a majority of the independent directors or an "all-independent" compensation committee. The CEO may not be present during voting or deliberations. Section 952 of the Dodd-Frank Act added a new Section 10C to the Exchange Act requiring the SEC to direct the national securities exchanges and associations to prohibit the listing of any equity security of a company unless all compensation committee members are independent and meet enhanced independence requirements.

Proof of compliance in corporate governance

Most companies have attained and surpassed the minimum requirements in SOX for independent directors. In recent years, it has become common that the company's CEO is the only non-independent director on the board. Recent studies of large public companies show
that more than 90% of boards today have two or fewer non-independent directors.[164]

The *2010 Spencer Stuart Board Index* showed the following results, all of which indicate that companies are taking the requirements for director independence seriously:[165]

- More than 40% of boards split the chair and CEO roles, and 19% of chairs are truly independent.

- 72% of boards now elect directors to one-year terms, up from 40% a decade ago.

- 71% of boards (up from 65% in 2009) require directors

who fail to secure a majority vote to offer their resignation.

- 71% of S&P 500 companies now limit other corporate directorships that directors may hold in some way (up from 27% in 2006).

- 62% of boards limit the number of other public company boards on which the company CEO may serve.

- Almost 75% of S&P 500 boards have adopted mandatory retirement policies for directors—up from 58% in 2000. (The retirement age is rising, however. 79% of boards set the age at 72 or older versus 37% in 2000. 19% set it at 75 or older, versus 1% in 2000.)

Listing standards affect growing influence of institutional investors

Since 2000, there has been an increasing trend away from individual stock ownership towards institutional ownership. While individuals directly held over 93% of U.S. equities in 1950, by 2006 that amount had fallen to approximately 33%, and by 2009, had decreased further to about 25%.[166]

In 2010, the NYSE adopted rules to eliminate broker discretionary voting in uncontested elections. Broker discretionary voting happens when brokers vote shares held on behalf of clients without other instructions. The Dodd-Frank Act eliminates broker discretionary voting on executive compensation and other significant matters to be determined by the SEC. Together, the NYSE and SEC rules will result in a greater ability for activist institutional shareholders to influence business actions, policies, and strategies at major public companies.

The growing influence of both institutional investors and proxy advisory firms has been a catalyst for the dramatic decline in public corporations' use of structural "defensive" measures, such as poison pills, actions that can be taken to make stock unattractive for potential purchasers.[167]

The increased influence of institutional investors and

proxy advisory firms, along with new regulatory obligations has changed the role and composition of the board itself. For example, the role of the board has changed from one focused primarily on working with management on the corporation's business and strategy to a board with a greater focus on monitoring and oversight.[168]

> For more information on director education programs, see www.nacdonline.org, the website for the National Association of Corporate Directors

Conclusion

Although SOX, the Dodd-Frank Act, and the listing standards overlap in many instances, directors of a company listed on the NYSE or NASDAQ (or other regional stock exchanges) must understand all applicable obligations. Corporations' management and directors have acknowledged the need to stay current with corporate governance best practices, leading to the proliferation of director education programs.

Proxy advisory services exist to advise institutional investors on their votes and on topics ranging from electing corporate directors to shareholder proposals. These proxy advisory services may develop new best practices annually. Board members who do not adhere to their best practice policies may not be recommended for reelection.

To assist companies with compliance related to the new rules and SOX generally, the NYSE (through Corporate Board Member, a NYSE company) and NASDAQ (through the National Association of Corporate Directors) have educational programs for board members.[169] The listing standards, much like SOX and the Dodd-Frank Act, have changed what governance means for public companies and has created the need for new directors with integrity and knowledge to fill new vacancies and become current on new governance developments.

7 | What Are the Additional Requirements for Members of Audit Committees?

GUEST CHAPTER AUTHOR: **Kimberly Zeoli,** Partner, Deloitte & Touche LLP, National Health Sciences Regulatory & Compliance Advisory Practice

Additional requirements apply to members of audit committees because the audit committee is an important subset of the corporation's board of directors, especially in U.S. public companies. The corporation's audit committee charter and relevant regulatory requirements determine what is expected of audit committee members.

This chapter provides a brief overview of some fundamental requirements for audit committees, but it is not an all-inclusive list of activities that an audit committee should or must execute to comply with the law. All corporations should consult with legal counsel regarding the applicability and implementation of regulatory requirements for specific audit committee activities.

Key responsibilities of the audit committee

In general, the audit committee is responsible for overseeing areas such as risk, compliance, internal controls, financial reporting, audit functions (internal and external), and monitoring activities.[170]

The audit committee's list of duties and responsibilities varies, depending upon the type, complexity, and size of the corporation. Key responsibilities of the committee usually include the following:

- Having an effective relationship with management;
- Working closely with the independent auditor to understand the auditor's activities and to identify and resolve issues;
- Overseeing dissemination of earnings press releases, financial information, and earnings guidance;
- Providing oversight to the internal audit function;
- Taking an effective approach to risk oversight and governance—particularly with respect to financial risks;
- Overseeing the establishment of appropriate internal controls and antifraud programs;
- Monitoring management of the code of ethics; and
- Establishing a process for investigating allegations of misconduct, especially those against senior management.

Some of these key responsibilities are described in more detail below.

Interaction with the external auditor

One of the audit committee's most important roles is managing the corporation's relationship with the corporation's external auditor (also commonly referred to as the "independent auditor"). This includes making recommendations to retain or replace the independent auditor. The audit committee meets with the independent auditor before and after the audit to discuss the scope of the work, any special procedures necessary, and issues encountered. The audit committee also reviews a letter to management from the independent auditor that summarizes audit observations.

Interaction with internal auditors

Another important role of the audit committee is oversight of the Director of Internal Audit and the Internal Audit Department. It is essential for this function to remain independent from the rest of the corporation, so that the director and the department can provide objective reviews in high risk areas of the company such as finance, accounting, purchasing, inventory, etc. The audit committee has several oversight responsibilities related to internal auditing, including assessing the director's performance, approving the annual internal audit plan, reviewing significant report findings, and receiving updates on improvement activities.

Risk oversight and governance

Not surprisingly, recent economic events continue to drive focus on the need for improved risk oversight, regardless of industry. In line with the SEC's new proxy disclosure requirement on board risk oversight, many boards are raising their expectations, asking senior executives to strengthen their risk management practices, understanding the corporation's portfolio of risks, and monitoring the enterprise's top risk exposures.[171]

Implementing an effective enterprise-wide risk management program is no small task. To add to the challenge, board oversight of management's risk management efforts is often delegated—in whole or in part—to the audit committee, which has a very full agenda already.

Given the demands on audit committees, members are asking for improvements and leading practices they can use to enhance their own processes. Audit committees are exploring methods for evaluating risk information to make sure that the appropriate top-down approach is implemented to obtain an enterprise view of risks. Boards are learning that Enterprise Risk Management is producing better risk insights to help corporations improve strategic oversight while simultaneously meeting new regulatory requirements.

Internal controls and antifraud programs

The audit committee needs to be comfortable that the

corporation has effective controls in place, as well as antifraud programs and policies to prevent and identify fraud. Consequently, the audit committee needs to understand whether key controls are in place and functioning properly, and that financial reporting risk areas have proper management oversight and approval processes. Inherent high risk areas traditionally require higher levels of approval authority and responsibility, including areas such as pricing and contracting, long term obligations, and large expenditures. In complex accounting areas, specialized technical skills are required for effective internal control—as is often the case with:

- Revenue recognition;
- Business combinations;
- Impairments;
- Leasing;
- Derivatives and hedging;
- Stock-based compensation;
- Financing arrangements; and
- Fair value measurements.

A corporation's internal control and antifraud programs are assessed by its independent auditor, internal auditors, and financial management personnel. These parties should be able to provide information to the audit committee about the extent to which internal controls and antifraud programs are operating effectively.

Code of ethics and Corporate Compliance Program

The audit committee also may be the board committee to confirm that the corporation has an effective ethics and compliance program in place and supported by a whistleblower hotline.

The U.S. Sentencing Commission's Federal Sentencing Guidelines, as noted previously in Chapter Three and as further discussed below, provide a foundation for establishing an effective corporate compliance program. Senior management involvement is required to maintain a strong corporate culture, commitment, and effective communications. Outside of formal policies and procedures, the company's culture needs to encourage the airing of complaints/challenges. Otherwise, the best processes will not be utilized when an employee has critical information that should be shared.

Another important role of the board, and in particular the audit committee, is to set and reinforce the appropriate "tone at the top." In this regard, the audit committee should be sure to encourage management to apply consistent and prompt consequences in instances of non-compliance with the code of ethics.

In each of the areas described above, there are additional considerations and applicable regulatory requirements that boards and audit committee members should consider in order to carry out their responsibilities. Perhaps the most basic step is for management and the board to provide the audit committee with the right level of knowledge through a continuing education program. Refer to *Tools and Resources for Audit Committees* at the end of this chapter for more information.

What is an audit committee not responsible for?

The audit committee's role is to provide reasonable oversight of management and the independent auditor. The audit committee should not perform the role of management. Very simply stated, the audit committee is not responsible for planning and conducting audits, determining the accuracy of financial statements in all material respects, or assuring the corporation's compliance with all applicable financial laws and regulations. However, the audit committee is responsible for providing the ultimate oversight for these important functions by reviewing, challenging, and advising management.

What does an audit committee look like?

Audit committees typically consist of three to five independent directors. As outlined in the previous chapter, NYSE and NASDAQ require audit committees to consist exclusively of independent directors. In any case, members of an audit committee should be independent of management and "disinterested"—free from relationships that would interfere with the exercise of independent judgment.

Audit committee members should (1) be financially literate and (2) have a sufficient understanding of financial reporting and monitoring principles to identify and address significant financial issues that may arise.

Seeking financial experts

SEC rules require a company to disclose whether it has at least one "audit committee financial expert" serving on its audit committee, and if so, the name of the expert and whether the expert is independent of management. A company that does not have an audit committee financial expert must disclose this fact and explain why it has no such expert.[172]

Who would qualify as an audit committee financial expert?

The SEC defines an audit committee financial expert as a person who has the following attributes:

- An understanding of generally accepted accounting principles and financial statements;

- The ability to assess the general application of such principles in connection with the accounting for estimates, accruals, and reserves;

- Experience preparing, auditing, analyzing, or evaluating financial statements that present a breadth and level of complexity of accounting issues that are generally comparable to the breadth and complexity of issues that can reasonably be expected to be raised by the registrant's financial statements, or experience actively supervising one or more persons engaged in such activities;

- An understanding of internal controls and procedures for financial reporting; and

- An understanding of audit committee functions.[173]

Under the SEC rules, a person must have acquired such attributes through any one or more of the following:

- Education and experience as a principal financial officer, principal accounting officer, controller, public accountant, or auditor or experience in one or more positions that involve the performance of similar functions

continues

Who would qualify as an audit committee financial expert?

continued

- Experience actively supervising a principal financial officer, principal accounting officer, controller, public accountant, auditor, or person performing similar functions;

- Experience overseeing or assessing the performance of companies or public accountants with respect to the preparation, auditing, or evaluation of financial statements; or

- Other relevant experience.[174]

An opportunity for financial experts

If you possess the required financial skills, volunteering to sit on the audit committee is a very good way to gain entry to a board of directors. As noted above, the SEC requires public companies to identify the financial experts serving on their audit committees. A study released in 2010 examined whether the skills and abilities necessary for service as a financial expert may have affected the push for gender diversity in the boardroom. Analysis of a sample of S&P 500 and Russell Microcap companies indicated that female participation in corporate governance has increased since 2003, but that the growth was attributable to smaller firms. Increases in women representation among large firms appears to have slowed dramatically. Few women were named as audit committee financial experts immediately after implementation of the SEC requirement, which arose from SOX. By 2009, however, the number and percentage of women financial experts had increased significantly, reaching levels comparable to those for corporate boards as a whole. The 2010 study found that gender diversity is not directly hampered by the specialized skills and experiences required of a financial expert.[175]

Although the opportunity for financial experts may be increasing, the latest wave of corporate scandals may lead some

> For a discussion of the liability facing directors in today's enforcement and litigation climate, see Chapter Three.

to conclude that serving on a board in general is too risky. On the other hand, some may prefer to serve on an audit committee in order to play a more significant role in fiduciary oversight of key high risk areas.

Audit committee vs. compliance committee, and the importance of corporate compliance programs

In general, corporations face an enormous challenge in dealing with a large variety of federal, state, and local statutes and regulations. Some boards have formed a separate committee of the board to provide oversight of the corporation's compliance program activities. Some corporations have a subcommittee called the "audit and compliance committee" to reflect these combined responsibilities. As compliance issues may overlap with the responsibilities of the audit committee, companies often have the company's chief compliance officer report to the audit committee. In other organizations, compliance oversight responsibilities may report to a separate committee of the board or a different standing committee of the board, for example, the governance committee, responsible for these matters.

To manage the risk of liability arising from this regulatory environment, it is recommended, and under certain circumstances required, to adopt and maintain an effective corporate compliance program. Such programs usually are designed in accordance with the standards for an effective compliance program under the Federal Sentencing Guidelines (FSG) established by the U.S. Sentencing Commission.[176] Under an effective compliance program, corporations can proactively address these risks before government enforcement and perhaps reduce overall liability exposure.

Corporations, like individuals, can be found guilty of criminal conduct, and the punishment for felonies and Class A misdemeanors is governed by Chapter 8 of the FSG. While corporations cannot be imprisoned, they can be:

- fined,
- sentenced to probation for up to five years,
- ordered to make restitution,

- required to issue public notices of conviction to their victims, and

- subject to forfeiture and debarment statutes.

Data collected by the U.S. Sentencing Commission reflects that corporations have been sentenced for a wide range of crimes such as fraud, environmental waste discharge, tax offenses, antitrust offenses, and food and drug violations. The Organizational Sentencing Guidelines (which apply to corporations, partnerships, labor unions, pension funds, trusts, non-profit entities, and governmental units) initially became effective November 1, 1991.[77]

> For the most current information, refer to the U.S. Sentencing Commission's FSG Manuals and proposed guideline amendments at www.ussc.gov.

Effective November 1, 2010, the U.S. Sentencing Commission's amendments (the 2010 Amendments) to its FSG Manual may have substantial impact on what constitutes effective compliance programs for organizations.[178] These amendments include a focus on: (1) board reporting relationships of the chief compliance officer; and (2) actions organizations should take following detection of criminal conduct.

The 2010 Amendments highlight the importance of comprehensive and effective compliance programs. Under the "direct report" requirement, the chief compliance officer must give regular reports directly to the board of directors. The compliance officer must report allegations of impropriety to the board promptly. The 2010 Amendments make it clear that an organization in which the chief compliance officer reports to the general counsel or to a corporate officer only, and not also to the board or a committee of the board, will be considered to have an ineffective structure. The 2010 Amendments also mandate that the board be educated on the importance of compliance and that compliance program effectiveness be continually evaluated.

The FSG assigns a culpability score to a criminally liable corporation based on company size, the management level at which the crime took place, and the effectiveness of the corporate compliance program. Under the FSG, the culpability score is lowered significantly if the corporation has an effective corporate compliance program. The Department of Justice principles on "charging a corporation" include a focus on the importance of corporate compliance programs. These charging principles question whether the corporate compliance program is well designed, is applied earnestly and in good faith, and whether the corporate compliance program works.[179]

The FSG requires that organizations establish an effective corporate compliance program through promoting an organizational culture that encourages ethical conduct and a commitment to compliance with the law. This program should include at a minimum the following seven elements:

(1) The organization shall establish standards and procedures to prevent and detect criminal conduct.

(2) The organization's governing authority shall be knowledgeable about the content and operation of the compliance and ethics program and shall exercise reasonable oversight with respect to the implementation and effectiveness of the compliance and ethics program.

High-level personnel of the organization shall ensure that the organization has an effective compliance and ethics program, as described in the FSG. Specific individual(s) within high-level personnel shall be assigned overall responsibility for the compliance and ethics program.

Specific individual(s) within the organization shall be delegated day-to-day operational responsibility for the compliance and ethics program. Individual(s) with operational responsibility shall report periodically to high-level personnel and, as appropriate, to the governing authority, or an appropriate subgroup of the governing authority, on the effectiveness of the compliance and ethics program. To carry out such operational responsibility, such individual(s) shall be given adequate resources, appropriate authority, and direct access to the governing authority or an appropriate subgroup of the governing authority.

(3) The organization shall use reasonable efforts not to include within the substantial authority personnel of the organization any individual whom the organization knew, or should have known through the exercise of due diligence, has engaged in illegal activities or other

conduct inconsistent with an effective compliance and ethics program.

(4) The organization shall take reasonable steps to communicate periodically and in a practical manner its standards and procedures, and other aspects of the compliance and ethics program, to the appropriate individuals by conducting effective training programs and otherwise disseminating information appropriate to such individuals' respective roles and responsibilities. These individuals include members of the governing authority, high-level personnel, substantial authority personnel, the organization's employees, and, as appropriate, the organization's agents.

(5) The organization shall take reasonable steps: to ensure that the organization's compliance and ethics program is followed, including monitoring and auditing to detect criminal conduct; to evaluate periodically the effectiveness of the organization's compliance and ethics program; and to have and publicize a system, which may include mechanisms that allow for anonymity or confidentiality, whereby the organization's employees and agents may report or seek guidance regarding potential or actual criminal conduct without fear of retaliation.

(6) The organization's compliance and ethics program shall be promoted and enforced consistently throughout the organization through: appropriate incentives to perform in accordance with the compliance and ethics program; and appropriate disciplinary measures for engaging in criminal conduct and for failing to take reasonable steps to prevent or detect criminal conduct.

(7) After criminal conduct has been detected, the organization shall take reasonable steps to respond appropriately to the criminal conduct and to prevent further similar criminal conduct, including making any necessary modifications to the organization's compliance and ethics program.[180]

A corporation that has properly adopted and implemented the seven elements above has a greater chance of showing that it has implemented an effective compliance program and will more likely face reduced penalties in event of a violation of the law.

For corporations in the health care and life sciences industry, the U.S. Department of Health and Human Services Office of the Inspector General (OIG) and The American Health Lawyers Association (AHLA) have co-sponsored a series of three papers on corporate responsibility and corporate compliance.[181] Each details the importance of having an effective corporate compliance program, as well as the role of board members as overseers. Although these papers were written before the 2010 Amendments and specifically for the U.S. health care and life sciences industry, the concepts in these papers also apply in other industry sectors. Directors should review these papers for potential leading practices.

The U.S. Department of Health and Human Services OIG website at http://oig.hhs.gov contains information and guidance on fraud prevention and detection, including a series of OIG compliance program guidance directed at the following segments of the health care industry:

- hospitals;
- clinical laboratories;
- home health agencies;
- third-party billing companies;
- the durable medical equipment, prosthetics, orthotics, and supply industry;
- hospices;
- Medicare Advantage (formerly known as Medicare+Choice) organizations;
- nursing facilities;
- ambulance suppliers;
- physicians; and
- pharmaceutical manufacturers.

Audit committee common and leading practices

The following list provides examples of common and leading practices for audit committees that go beyond what may be proscribed in legal/regulatory requirements.[182] The following list is not intended to be all-inclusive:

■ Perform an annual self-assessment of audit committee performance by having each member complete a performance evaluation questionnaire/scorecard and gather additional feedback from individuals that interact with audit committee;

■ Provide orientation to new members with committee members, executives, and internal auditors. Materials should include information on the company's history and operations, corporate governance, audit committee requirements and charter, recent financials and regulatory filings, industry trends, accounting policies and practices, company policies and the code of ethics, and significant business and financial risks;

■ Conclude each regular audit committee meeting with an executive session of the committee without members of management present;

■ Consider and plan the succession and/or rotation of audit committee members frequently;

■ Be briefed on key reports submitted by the company to any governmental body or to the public as needed;

■ In consultation with the independent auditor and the internal audit function, review the integrity of the company's financial statement reporting processes (both internal and external) and the internal control structure (including disclosure controls and procedures and internal control over financial reporting) on a quarterly basis;

■ Review the various annual internal, external, and compliance plans with relevant parties on a timely basis;

■ Review and advise on the selection or removal of the chief internal audit executive, chief compliance officer, and/or chief risk officer as appropriate;

■ Review the activities, organizational structure, and funding of the internal audit/compliance/risk functions, as well as the qualifications of personnel;

■ Review the internal audit and compliance office charters and recommend any changes that may be necessary; **101**

- Annually review the company's code of ethical conduct and the company's systems to monitor compliance with and enforcement of this code, including whether the code remains in compliance with applicable rules and regulations;
- Periodically receive and review reports of code violations and how they were identified and treated;
- With the independent auditors, the internal audit function, and management, review the extent to which changes or improvements in financial or accounting practices, as approved by the audit committee, have been implemented annually; and
- Participate in appropriate continuing education designed for audit committee members.

Sample Tools and Resources for Audit Committees

- The American Institute of Certified Public Accountants (AICPA) Audit Committee Toolkit includes: *Audit Committee Financial Expert Decision Tree, Discussions to Expect from the Independent Auditor, Guidelines for Hiring the Chief Audit Executive,* and more. This publication is available at www.aicpa.org.
- The Institute of Internal Auditors (IIA) offers several publications for board and audit committee members, including *The Audit Committee: Internal Audit Oversight Implementing Best Practices and High Standards,* available at www.theiia.org.
- The Resources section of the Association of Certified Fraud Examiners' website includes articles on whistleblower hotlines. Visit www.acfe.com.
- Articles on board evaluation, improving director effectiveness, and other hot topics can be found on the National Association of Corporate Directors (NACD) website at www.nacdonline.org.
- The latest research, information, and tools for directors and board committees can be found on Deloitte's Center for Corporate Governance website at www.corpgov.deloitte.com.[183]

8 What Additional Duties and Risks Face a Director on the Board of a Non-Profit Corporation?

WITH CONTRIBUTIONS FROM **Jesse M. Caplan**,
Epstein Becker & Green, P.C.

Whether a company is organized as a for profit or non-profit corporation, the directors have the responsibility to promote the best interests of the corporation and to fulfill their fiduciary duties. Directors of non-profit corporations also are responsible for ensuring that the actions of the corporation further the non-profit organization's charitable mission. As a result, non-profit directors have not only a duty of loyalty and duty of care, but also a unique duty of obedience, as explained below.

What interests do non-profit directors serve?

Non-profit directors may be elected by existing directors, the board of a corporate member, or by the beneficiary constituency of the non-profit corporation. Identifying whose interest to serve is not as easy for non-profit directors as it is for their for profit counterparts. After all, non-profit corporations do not have shareholders. A non-profit director's fiduciary duty is owed to the corporation's best interest and to the organization's charitable mission.

Do the definitions of "Duty of Care" and "Duty of Loyalty" change for non-profits?

Like their for profit counterparts, directors of a non-profit corporation must demonstrate that they are fulfilling their duty of care—acting as a person in a similar position would reasonably act. However, the non-profit laws in at least twelve states include additional requirements for procedures to validate "interested" transactions and the burden of proof of an interested transaction's validity.[184] In most states, the state Attorney General has the authority and responsibility to monitor and oversee charitable organizations.

See Chapter Three for more on interested director transactions and the duty of loyalty.

The duty of loyalty takes on an additional element with non-profit corporations. Non-profit directors' duty of loyalty includes compliance with the federal tax code. The federal tax code prohibits "private inurement" (private benefit) from the activities of federal tax-exempt organizations. Specifically, no part of the earnings of a tax-exempt organization may "inure to the benefit of any private shareholder or individual."[185] If a director benefits, the director may have breached his or her duty of loyalty. Private inurement can place the corporation's federal tax-exempt status in jeopardy as well. Beyond that, if a particular transaction results in an economic benefit to an "insider" (including a director), and the transaction does not meet the requirements for the rebuttable presumption of reasonableness, a director receiving the benefit or approving that transaction could be personally liable for excise tax penalties.

A step that all boards can take to ensure compliance with the duty of loyalty is to implement a comprehensive conflict of interest policy. The Internal Revenue Service (IRS) has issued sample policies, including particular procedures to address potential conflicts of interest.[186] These policies should be part of the corporation's overall corporate compliance program. Conflicts of interest policies should be reviewed regularly and revised, as appropriate, in light of the ever-changing corporate responsibility environment for all boards of directors.

Case Examples: Fiduciary Duties

One of the most famous cases addressing fiduciary duties of care in a non-profit health care context is *Queen of Angels Hospital v. Younger*.[187] In *Queen of Angels*, a hospital's Catholic sponsor claimed it was owed sixteen million dollars for past services rendered by its nuns to the hospital. The hospital board subsequently settled with the sponsor, agreeing to pay $200 per month for each nun over the age of seventy, whether or not the nun had worked at the hospital. The California Court of Appeals held that the directors of the hospital breached their fiduciary duties because they had no reasonable basis for believing in the validity of the claim. The court reasoned that, although the sponsor's claim for compensation was made in good faith, both the sponsor and the hospital considered the services rendered by the nuns to be donations, and therefore the hospital had no legal obligation to pay the claim. Accordingly, the hospital's board had not exercised sound business judgment and had breached its fiduciary duties by agreeing to pay. This case illustrates that, even in a non-profit context, when determining whether directors have violated their duty of care, courts will focus on the board's underlying decision-making process.

One of the seminal cases discussing fiduciary duties for directors of non-profit corporations is *Stern v. Lucy Webb Hayes National Training School for Deaconesses & Missionaries* (known as *Sibley Hospital*).[188] In *Sibley Hospital*, plaintiffs brought a class action lawsuit against a variety of defendants, including individual trustees, alleging that members of a hospital board of trustees breached their fiduciary duties of loyalty by mismanaging hospital funds. Board trustees had instructed Sibley Hospital to deposit hospital funds in non-interest bearing accounts at financial institutions in which the trustees had interests. The plaintiffs pointed to evidence demonstrating that the trustees failed to disclose those individual interests. The United States District Court for the District of Columbia held that the trustees breached their duties of

continues

Case Examples: Fiduciary Duties

continued

care and loyalty because they were grossly negligent in failing to supervise properly the corporation's investments (the duty of care) and in engaging in self-dealing transactions (the duty of loyalty).

Despite its holding, the *Sibley Hospital* court declined to award damages. Instead, the court required that each newly-elected trustee read the court's opinion and the related order, and that proof of that reading be set forth in a signed document or meeting minutes. The court also ordered that, at least a week prior to each meeting of the full board, the trustees receive a formal written statement prepared by the hospital's treasurer, disclosing in detail the full extent of all hospital business with any bank or other financial institution since the last meeting. Finally, the court ordered each trustee to disclose to the board, prior to regularly scheduled meetings, any affiliations with banks or other financial institutions.

What is the duty of obedience?

The duty of obedience requires the directors of a non-profit organization to remain faithful to the charitable mission and purposes of that non-profit organization. Directors will find these charitable purposes in the corporation's articles of incorporation or organizational charter. The duty of obedience arises because donors rely on the corporation to use gifts for the corporation's stated mission. The diversion of corporation financial resources to other goals, even other charitable goals, is unlawful. Some non-profits—like tax-exempt hospitals—must satisfy the community benefit standard, which requires that the entity justify its tax-exempt status by providing a quantifiable benefit to its community.[189]

Non-profit corporations may engage in activities unrelated to the organization's charitable purpose, including commercial activities, so long as the organization is *primarily* engaged in activities that further its charitable purpose.[190] However, these unrelated business activities may result in taxable "unrelated business income."[191]

Non-profit directors, with their duty of obedience, encounter a more difficult and complex decision-making process than do directors of for profit corporations, who are subject only to the duties of care and loyalty. In a merger or other business transaction, for example, it may be appropriate for the directors of a non-profit hospital to accept a lower bid from one of several suitors because the chosen bidder would provide a far higher level of public benefit or service to the community.

Case Example: The Duty of Obedience

The duty of obedience has formed the legal basis for substantial litigation involving non-profit corporations. A prime example is *In re Manhattan Eye, Ear & Throat Hospital (MEETH)*[192] The decision in *MEETH* noted that the duty of obedience requires a director of a non-profit corporation to "'be faithful to the purposes and goals of the [corporation],' since '[u]nlike business corporations, whose ultimate objective is to make money, non-profit corporations are defined by their specific objectives: perpetuation of particular activities are central to the *raison d'être* of the organization.'" [193]

What conduct would breach the duty of obedience?

Although the answer to this question varies depending on the circumstances, the following examples illustrate the types of conduct that might constitute a breach of the duty of obedience:

- Failure to monitor legal changes in the requirements for tax-exempt status;
- Failure to monitor the activities of employees and agents to ensure that their actions are true to the company's charitable mission;
- Failure to monitor the use of the corporation's funds to ensure that such funds are used to support mission; or
- An unauthorized change or expansion of the corporation's activities outside of the corporation's stated charitable mission.

Does the business judgment rule apply to non-profit corporations?

The conventional wisdom is that directors of non-profit corporations enjoy certain protections against liability, including the business judgment rule, similar to those applicable to for profit corporation directors. If evidence demonstrates that directors met their duties of care and loyalty and took into account the corporation's charitable mission, the business judgment rule operates as a shield from personal liability—even if the board's decision was unfavorable to the corporation.

For an introduction to the business judgment rule, see Chapter Three.

The rationale behind the business judgment rule is the same for both for profit and non-profit corporations: It encourages rational risk-taking and innovation. It also limits litigation and unfair exposure, encourages quality directors to serve, and limits the intrusion of the judicial system into corporate governance.

What is the risk of state enforcement against non-profit directors?

Non-profit directors face three principal types of enforcement actions—criminal enforcement actions, civil enforcement actions, and tax assessments. Criminal prosecution generally is limited to the most egregious violations. This might include conduct similar to criminal conduct in a for profit corporation, such as egregious environmental liability, or negligence resulting in bodily harm. Consequently, most enforcement actions for breaches of fiduciary duties by non-profit directors are civil actions seeking either damages or orders to prevent future violations.

State attorneys general have the authority to bring actions on behalf of the state to preserve the assets of charitable, non-profit corporations located in their jurisdictions. In most states, the state attorney general has either sole or primary standing to take action against directors of non-profit corporations for breaches of fiduciary duty.

Many commentators believe that the substantial increase in the number of non-profit corporations, the sophistication of their operations, and the broad manner in which they affect the public has led to a corresponding rise in recent fiduciary duty enforcement activity. It is difficult to determine the extent of enforcement activities and state oversight—these proceedings generally are not public. In some cases, the state does not want these proceedings to become public as it may "chill" donations from the public to the charity. Nevertheless, it appears that litigation remains rare.

Can and Should Directors of Non-Profits be Compensated?

Unlike directors of for profit corporations, the vast majority of members of boards of directors of non-profit corporations serve without compensation, except for possible reimbursement of expenses related to their board work. Indeed, board members of public charities, a particular type of non-profit organization, typically are expected to donate both their time and money to the organization.

However, non-profit corporations that require board members with particular business expertise, and those that compete with for profit corporations in complex or highly regulated industries, may need to compensate directors for their board service. Compensation may be necessary to recruit and retain highly qualified, experienced, and committed individuals. In determining whether to compensate directors, non-profit boards should consider the following factors:

- whether compensation of board members is permitted under applicable state law and the organization's governing documents;

- whether compensation of board members is necessary and justified for this particular organization;

- how the level of compensation will be determined, and whether it is reasonable;

- whether the board has an inherent conflict of interest, and, if so, how the conflict will be addressed and mitigated; and

- whether there will be unintended consequences, including negative public reaction or risk to the organization's charitable status or charitable immunity.

continues

109

Can and Should Directors of Non-Profits be Compensated? (cont'd)

continues

The Panel on the Nonprofit Sector's *Principles for Good Governance and Ethical Practice, A Guide for Charities and Foundations* (October 2007, available at www.nonprofit panel.org) offers guidance on addressing non-profit board compensation issues (see Principle 20) as well as other non-profit governance questions. In light of the enhanced scrutiny of non-profit governance practices by the IRS, state attorneys general, and the public, non-profit boards considering board compensation should document and archive such documentation of these recommended factors.

What role does the IRS play in governing non-profit boards?

The benefit of tax-exempt status brings increased accountability and potential enforcement against a non-profit corporation and its directors—either by the IRS or by state attorneys general who have jurisdiction over the charitable assets of the non-profit corporation. To obtain charity tax-exempt status, a non-profit corporation must satisfy IRS requirements. Most importantly, the organization must be organized and operated exclusively for one of the charitable purposes set forth in the Internal Revenue Code, and its earnings may not "inure to the benefit of any private shareholder or individual."[194] Failure to pass the "operation" or "private inurement" tests can result in excise tax penalties or a loss of tax exemption.

The private inurement doctrine prohibits a tax-exempt organization from engaging in excess benefit transactions with insiders of the organization.[195] An excess benefit transaction occurs when the tax-exempt organization provides an economic benefit to an insider that exceeds the value of consideration received in exchange for providing that benefit.[196] Typically, insiders are officers, directors, managers, or others in a position to exercise control over the tax-exempt organization. Tax-exempt entities that engage in excess benefit transactions must disclose these transactions to the IRS.[197]

Excess benefit transactions may trigger intermediate sanctions. Intermediate sanctions consist of excise taxes that may be assessed against both the insider and "managers" approving the transaction.[198] Significantly, the personal liability for a non-profit director in an excess benefit transaction can be twofold: (1) the director could be an insider who receives an excess benefit, or (2) the director could be a manager who knowingly approved the transaction with another insider. Directors can reduce the risk of being involved in, or approving, excess benefit transactions by following effective board conflict of interest procedures and ensuring that potentially conflicted transactions meet the IRS's conditions for creating a "rebuttable presumption" that payments are reasonable. This test generally requires that:

- the decision-making body is composed entirely of individuals who do not have a conflict of interest with respect to the transaction;

- the body relies on external data showing fair market value; and

- the body adequately and contemporaneously documents the basis for its determination.[199]

How can non-profit directors manage these risks?

As described in Chapter Four, most states' laws permit for profit and non-profit corporations to limit a board member's personal liability in order to encourage board membership. By law, the corporation may indemnify its directors and officers against certain liabilities.

These "liability shield" laws protect uncompensated non-profit directors and officers from acts or omissions committed in the scope of their duties within the non-profit corporation.[200] Even if they are compensated, directors may be protected by D&O insurance, indemnification, and the business judgment rule.

What Sarbanes-Oxley means for non-profit corporations

As non-profit corporations are not publicly traded, most provisions of the Sarbanes-Oxley Act do *not* apply to non-profit corporations. A few SOX provisions do apply—for example, those relating to the penalties for obstruction of justice. [201]

For a detailed discussion of Sarbanes-Oxley and its implications, see Chapter Five.

Nevertheless, voluntary compliance with SOX and other federal, state, and private *SOX-like* standards can lead to significant and practical benefits. For example, a non-profit corporation that adopts SOX-like provisions may be able to procure D&O insurance at favorable terms. Non-profit organizations may face pressure to fulfill some SOX requirements to exhibit "good corporate governance practices." These demands and expectations may originate from a number of sources, including insurers, institutional investors, bond rating agencies, and state laws and regulations.[202] In the context of tax-exempt financing, rating agencies, bond insurers, and other parties generally have required non-profits to conform to many of the SOX requirements.

Some SOX provisions are best practices for non-profit corporations. Enacting any of these provisions could lead to better governance, as well as increased credibility and accuracy of non-profit financial statements. See Chapter Five for specifics.

New IRS Forms 1023 and 990—Increased scrutiny of board governance and independence

In the wake of SOX, the IRS has increased its oversight of tax-exempt organizations, including emphasis on financial disclosures, conflicts of interest, and board governance and independence. The IRS is increasing scrutiny on potential new non-profits, as well as existing non-profits.

In 2004, the IRS released an updated Form 1023. This is the form non-profits use to apply for exempt status. The form requires additional information regarding the potential non-profit organization's compensation structure, as well as its conflict of interest policy.

For tax years beginning in 2008, the IRS redesigned the Form 990—the tax return required to be filed by tax-exempt organizations—with particular focus on non-profit governance and transparency. These revisions apply many SOX-like disclosure and certification requirements. As a result, the new Form 990 requires additional information about:

- the independence of voting members of the board;
- family and business relationships among board members, officers, and key employees; and
- whether the corporation has adopted and followed good governance practices, like conflict of interest policies for avoiding insider transactions and procedures for reviewing and setting executive compensation.

While the Form 990 is a disclosure document and does not mandate how to manage a non-profit, it does provide a road map of what the IRS considers to be good non-profit governance practices and, therefore, how to reduce the potential for an IRS audit. A non-profit corporation's Form 990 filing is a public document. Prospective directors of non-profit organizations should review the corporation's filing to understand better how the corporation is operated and what governance practices the IRS may expect.[203]

Conclusion

Serving on the board of a non-profit organization offers the rewards and satisfaction of being part of a mission-driven enterprise. However, directors of non-profit organizations should consider the additional obligations and increased scrutiny that comes with governing a charitable corporation. Through conscientious focus on the organization's purpose and mission; on directors' duties of care, loyalty, and obedience; and on IRS best practices for non-profit governance, a non-profit board can reduce or avoid the attendant risks, while contributing to the greater good.

Becoming A
Great Director

9 The Board Search: How Do You Best Prepare and Position Yourself?

GUEST CHAPTER AUTHOR:
Kathleen Fehling, President, K. Fehling & Associates

With contributions by Lori Christiansen, Biotech Practice Leader, K. Fehling & Associates and Martha Stachitas, Vice President, K. Fehling & Associates

A corporation's search for a new member of its board continues to be an enigma to many prospective board candidates. Even under today's increasing scrutiny, it is estimated that 85% of all board seats are filled via the informal networking of existing board members and company management, leaving only 15% of new board seats are filled through retained executive search firms. Virtually all non-profit organizations, emerging companies, and private companies continue to rely upon the personal networks of the CEO and other board members to find and recruit new board members. Other than very large national headquarter organizations, such as the American Red Cross, non-profit companies typically recruit local community leaders to their boards of directors. Emerging companies, particularly in the high tech and life sciences industry, usually have boards predominately comprised of investors (venture capitalists or private investors) while other private companies, regardless of size, most often are filled with board members known to the CEO or other board members through years of business affiliations or longstanding personal relationships. In a family-owned company, typically a number of corporate directors will be family members. The 15% of board searches completed via retained executive search firms are primarily for mid-sized and larger public companies. Once a company has decided to retain a search firm to find a new corporate director, the specifications for that search usually are defined carefully and therefore, a much smaller pool of potential candidates will qualify.

To maximize networking opportunities, executives seeking board seats should have a solid understanding of these statistics. Be prepared to clearly articulate what you can bring to a board, identify the types of companies that will best suit your skills, and build a broad network of key contacts associated with those companies. Additionally, potential directors should target the 15% of those board seats filled via recruiters by introducing themselves to the retained search consultants with active board practices in the industry of focus.

Board search: Traditional board candidate

The most highly recruited board candidates are primarily current and former CEOs, and secondarily current and former CFOs. CEOs bring overall general management experience, credibility, name caché and respective career industry/market experience. CFOs have become highly recruited members of boards in this millennium, particularly within the public company sector, because of their capacity to lead audit and compensation committees (provided they meet SEC qualifications). Division Presidents and/or Division CFOs will not typically meet board qualifications unless they have had extensive experience within the desired market or Wall Street (if public company), or unless they meet other desired criteria.

Boards increasingly will be scrutinized to ensure that the directors as a whole represent shareholder and marketplace demographics. As mentioned in Chapter Ten, in February 2010, the SEC announced a new rule that requires the country's 15,000 publicly-traded companies to disclose to their shareholders via proxy statements whether they have a diversity policy for identifying and nominating candidates for their corporate board seats. This new SEC rule also requires companies to assess the effectiveness of the company's board diversity policy. Although the most common definition of diversity comprises gender, ethnicity, or country of origin, the SEC left room in its definition to include differences in professional experience, education, skill, and other attributes that contribute to a heterogeneous board. Nonetheless, in recruiting new board members, selection criteria are likely to include gender and ethnicity, particularly as public companies begin to report the success of their organizations' policies relative to this new SEC rule. Additionally, if a company is marketing products and/or services around the world, executives who are from non-U.S. countries and/or have spent significant time leading markets outside of the United States may be considered particularly desirable board candidates.

In summary, gaining your first seat on a for profit company's board likely will be challenging and therefore requires targeted effort and planning.

Understanding your strengths

Regardless of whether you have served in the role of CEO or CFO or in another capacity (e.g., legal, marketing, operations, human resources), it is critical that you have a clear understanding of what skills you would bring to a board—and therefore which companies would benefit most from your experience. Other than the CEO or CFO of an independent company, board consideration usually is reserved for those with functional or General Manager expertise reporting to the most senior level within a company—usually the CEO's executive staff. Companies seeking an external director usually choose to add expertise identified as lacking either within the company and/or the board. Priority is placed on recruiting an executive whose personality aligns well with the culture of the existing board. Therefore, board candidates should understand what capabilities they have to offer a board, and then target companies with parallel needs.

Board candidates should understand their strengths in three areas: (1) function, (2) industry, and (3) culture, as illustrated in the chart to follow.

Understanding Your Strengths

FUNCTION	INDUSTRY	CULTURE
■ CEO, President, General Manager	■ Pharmaceutical	■ Personality
■ Finance, CFO	■ Provider	■ Mission
■ Legal	■ Services	■ Vision
■ Sales/Marketing	■ Medical Device	■ Compensation
■ Research & Development	■ Biotechnology	■ Entrepreneurial
■ Operations	■ Consumer Products	■ Turn-Around
■ Clinical/Regulatory	■ Financial Services	■ High-Growth
■ Medical Affairs	■ Information Technology	
■ Human Resources	■ Other	

Certain board candidate experiences may be particularly beneficial where a candidate's past experiences parallels a company's plans to move forward in a similar way. Examples of experiences that should be highlighted as strengths if the board candidate has been intimately involved include:

- Completion of an Initial Public Offering (IPO)
- Spin-out of a public company
- Private equity transaction—public to private, or acquisition from a larger company
- Merger or integration of acquisition, especially if outside of the United States (OUS)
- International—specific geographic expertise, particularly if candidate resided OUS and ran OUS-business
- Development or commercialization of a specific technology or market

- Global supply chain/distribution expertise—especially in a high-growth, expanding company
- Family-owned public or private expertise
- High growth—$0 to $100 million for an emerging company, or $100 million to $2 billion or more for a larger company
- Turn-around—dramatic with impressive results (usually more than one)
- M&A—due diligence, deal and/or integration experience
- Legal expertise—DOJ, Food and Drug Administration (FDA), specific to industry.

Understanding these areas of strength is particularly critical as you start planning your effort to pursue your first board position. For example, some industries come under increased government enforcement and scrutiny. An executive who has led a company successfully through an investigation may prove to be beneficial to a board if he or she also is the right cultural fit (this could be the scenario where a general counsel becomes a non-traditional board candidate).
Another example of a board candidate leveraging his or her strength is when a company seeking to commercialize a novel technology seeks one non-investor board member with expertise in that specific industry space (often a highly specialized research and development or sales and marketing executive). A company seeking to expand outside of the United States will need and respect expertise within targeted countries, especially if that executive hails from the same industry or a parallel industry. A company spinning off its parent into a private or public entity will benefit from a board member who has experienced a spinoff with another company.
In summary, evaluate your strengths to prepare to match them with targeted companies.

Know your limitations

After evaluating the strengths you will bring to a board, ensure that you have reviewed your limitations as well.

- **Conflict with Current Position:** Executives usually are limited by their employer or current board of directors relative to the number and/or type of board they are permitted to serve. It can be awkward to accept an invitation to serve on a board and then later be forced to rescind when your current board or employer rejects the arrangement. Be sure to ask first. Some companies only allow executives to serve on non-profit boards. Some will allow private board seats, but not public. Many companies limit executives to one external seat (whether public or private, for profit or non-profit). Some companies will have an unforeseen conflict with the board position, such as competing product lines, a pending or current licensing deal, etc. (See Chapter Ten to read more about the trends relating to allowing executives to serve on external boards.)

- **Geographic location:** Serving on a board of directors requires commitment. Attendance at board meetings is mandatory. Ensure that you are able to attend at least 75% of the meetings, with a goal of attending 100%. Consider the location of the company and calculate travel time to and from board meetings, as coast-to-coast travel will make a considerable difference.

- **Functional and Industry Expertise:** Understand your functional and industry experience and the relevancy of those experiences to the company you are targeting. For example, if you have served as Vice President, Sales and Marketing or Vice President, Research and Development of a company that has commercialized an emerging technology from concept through FDA approvals and launch, another emerging company in a similar industry will find your skills valuable. However, most emerging technology companies are Venture Capital-funded. Typically, investors carry 90% of the board seats. Therefore, your previous success must be compelling, relative and parallel to the targeted company's future success. Functional and industry area of expertise are where executives tend to overestimate their actual expertise, especially as they advance higher in an organization. For example, executives may claim industries are similar and determine, "I can add to that company by just being on the board because I have such broad experience or because I come from a much larger company." The latter is a real miscue and has lost many a board seat for prospective directors. Other than former CFOs, for whom skills needed by a board's audit committee and the like are easily transferrable, functional area executives would be wise to know and clearly define specifically what expertise they will bring to the desired company as a board member.

▪ **Public vs. Private:** While many private companies follow public board governance guidelines, private companies are not required to do so and, in fact, because private companies are not required to report revenues, earnings, compensation or any of the other mandatory filings of a public company, risk is *typically* higher for a corporate director of a public company. However, prospective board candidates should be cautious of a private company that lacks structured corporate governance, as the lack thereof produces inherent risk to the prospective board member. Additionally, a private board that lacks structure and/or sophistication may not provide an environment conducive for an engaging board experience.

Finding and targeting the right board for you

Match your strengths and your limitations with the kinds of companies (and thus boards) that will most closely align with what you can contribute. First-time board members should evaluate opportunities with non-profit organizations, as well as with private and public companies, honing in on the type of company and segment that best fits with his or her experience. The chart **Choosing a Board: What to Expect** provides a general overview of the company segments, board compensation, and search parameters.

Choosing a Board: What to Expect

Non-profit Companies	■ Can be viewed as a good way to gain board of director experience, but not viewed as equal experience as a for profit board ■ Potential access to for profit board of directors if members are strong industry leaders ■ Usually no compensation; when joining, be sure to clarify financial contribution/fundraising requirements of board members
Early Stage Private Companies	■ Excellent board of director experience ■ If venture-capital backed, domain experience typically is required ■ Low or no cash compensation, board members typically paid in equity only
Mid to Large Private Companies	■ Excellent board of director experience ■ Ensure you have a cultural fit with the company as there is less external oversight ■ Ensure board structure and sophistication ■ Compensation can be "all over the board"
All Sizes of Public Companies	■ Public seats are the majority of the 15% board seats filled by retained executive search ■ Historical focus on candidates with CEO or CFO experience ■ Candidates must meet Nominating & Governance Committee criteria for outside directors ■ Compensation in cash and stock depending upon the size of the company

Additional considerations

There are several areas that merit serious consideration when evaluating a possible board opportunity. Those eager to serve as a corporate director should pay particular attention to the following areas:

- **Risk assessment:** Board service comes with the risk of liability in both private and public companies of all sizes and growth stages. Do not rely on the presence of other sophisticated executives on the board as an indicator that the level of risk is acceptable. You need to judge risk yourself. As described in Chapter 4, ensure that the company has adequate D&O insurance in place and that the policy is paid and current. The risks and adequacy of D&O insurance are particularly acute in the case of a thinly financed, friends and family or angel-financed company; in a company with inexperienced founders; and where adequate legal counsel has not been engaged to formally structure the company at an early stage. Have your personal attorney review and advise you about the risk relative to your personal situation. You may be advised to seek additional liability protection. Sometimes, companies appreciate having issues regarding the D&O policy brought to the leadership's attention during the recruitment process, so that the company can update its policy, if needed.

> For more information on D&O insurance and risk management, see Chapter Four. For more information about the possible liabilities of board service, see Chapter Three.

- **Expectations:** Define, discuss, and communicate your expectations, observations, and concerns before accepting a position. Be sure to conduct adequate due diligence around board members as well as the key executives leading the company. Address and discuss any red flags. Make sure your expectations for your areas of contribution are well-aligned with those of other board members. This is especially true for those brought onto the board for particular areas of expertise, such as finance.

If you desire your contribution to be broader, determine the likelihood upfront so potential conflict is avoided down the road.

- **Board relationships:** Assess the company and board's likely focus and probable decisions necessary during your tenure. One common occurrence in a private company moving towards commercialization is the replacement of a founding CEO for an experienced CEO. This can be a challenging time for the company and a strain on the board. If your primary relationship is with the founder(s), ask yourself how well you will serve if faced with this governance situation or something similar.

- **Long-term fit with career:** Review the impact of board service on your ability to best manage your career and any existing or pending contractual limitations relative to your tenure and for any board seat. Will a merger or partner of this company conflict with your current career or vice versa (your current employer merges or partners with a competitor of this company's, for example)? When selecting a board, be sure that the fit is close enough to your expertise that you are able to be an integral productive member of the board but not too close that you are forced to exclude yourself from key board meetings due to a conflict with your current employer (a pending merger, partnership or new product launch where you hold key information). and exchange of confidential information?

- **Non-profit boards:** Determine exactly what the board expects of your contribution. Is the director simply providing advisory oversight, or are you expected to make an annual contribution and/or conduct specified fundraising for the organization? Determine whether there will be a capital campaign planned during your tenure and, if so, what will be expected of you.

Conclusion

As a first time member of any board, you want the experience to be one that will be satisfying both personally and professionally. Board relationships are long-term and the network of influence from other board members is broad. Be sure you can deliver upon your commitment.

10 What Is the Business Case for Gender Diversity in the Boardroom, and What Will It Take to Achieve It?

GUEST CHAPTER AUTHOR:
Eleanor R. Whitley, Executive Director, WBL Foundation

We have all heard some version of the dismal statistics about gender diversity in the boardroom. Women hold only 15.7% of Fortune 500 board seats.[204] Sixty-one Fortune 500 companies have no women on their corporate boards.[205] Only sixty-two Fortune 500 boards have more than two women on the board.[206] In the years since Sarbanes-Oxley and since the original publication of this book, U.S. corporations have continued to elect new corporate directors "like it's 1999."

Says T.K. Kerstetter, President and CEO, Board Member, Inc., "The challenge in today's business world is to recognize a person not as a 'good woman director' but as a 'good director.' It shouldn't be an issue of gender or race, but of qualification."[207] Unfortunately, it is difficult to heed this good advice when the percentages of women on corporate boards remain stagnant, as illustrated in **State of the Research: Women's Roles on Boards Stagnant,** below.

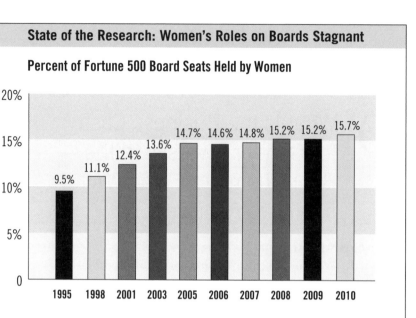

State of the Research: Women's Roles on Boards Stagnant

Percent of Fortune 500 Board Seats Held by Women

Source: Research © Catalyst, compiled from annual Catalyst Census documents, available at www.catalyst.org.

Unable or unwilling to wait for the business case for board diversity to take hold, countries around the world have begun acknowledging the benefits of gender diversity. Many countries have taken the lawmaking route by enacting statutes that mandate gender diversity on corporate boards. See the diagram below, **Where Does Your Country Fall on the Gender Diversity Mandate Spectrum?,** for an overview of the international range of mandates, requirements, and requests regarding gender diversity in corporate board service.)

Where Does Your Country Fall on the Gender Diversity Mandate Spectrum?

APPROACH	COUNTRY	EFFECTIVE DATE
Country has specifics about when the search process must identify women candidates	Israel	1993
Country mandates a percentage of the board should be women, generally	Norway (40%)	2008
	Iceland (40%)	2013
	Spain (40%)	2015
	France (40%)	2016*
	European Union (20%)	Proposed*
Country requires companies to explain their lack of board diversity	Australia	2010
Country requires explanations of board composition in some circumstances	United States	2010
	United Kingdom	2010

*Legislation pending.

Source: Catalyst, "Quick Takes," www.catalyst.org/publication/433/women-on-boards.

While a legal mandate may not be the right solution for the United States, in the face of recession and economic scandal, companies increasingly must focus on good corporate governance. Good corporate governance is not possible without the right people in the room. Women should be included in the boardroom not because of some ethereal belief that diversity is the right thing to do. Rather, women should be included because diversity creates a board that better represents a company—its employees, its customers, and the vendors with whom the company works. Most importantly, gender diversity is necessary because studies have shown that boards with more gender diversity have better debates, make better decisions, are more likely to follow policies and procedures, and are more likely to make money.

Common sense tells us that a board should reflect customers, shareholders, etc. But for those who cannot see past the numbers, what are the practical business reasons to be sure boardrooms include at least three board members representing each gender?

The business case: Women on board bring better form, function, and results

Why is it important to have women on corporate boards? Simply put, it is so that they can make a positive difference by providing diverse perspectives from their male counterparts. However, research shows that a woman director continues to serve alone or with just one other woman.[208] Women on boards including two or fewer women experienced feelings of tokenism and stereotyping. To find the true success story of gender diversity—a woman on the board being heard, having impact, and affecting the bottom line—the board should include three or more women.

Boards with *three or more* women had a noticeably different dynamic, one where gender "becomes a non-issue."[209] The groundbreaking 2006 report by the Wellesley Centers for Women, *Critical Mass on Corporate Boards: Why Three or More Women Enhance Governance*, described interviews and discussions with fifty women directors, twelve CEOs, and seven corporate secretaries from Fortune 1000 companies. One woman director said: "One woman is the invisibility phase; two women is the conspiracy phase; three women is mainstream."[210] The study describes, with quotes and detail, the "difficult issues and problems" that are not ignored, the "open and collaborative boardroom dynamic," and a quicker timetable on realizing problems and issues because of the differentiation of opinions.[211] The study demonstrated that a critical mass of three or more women can cause a fundamental change in the boardroom and enhance corporate governance.

Canadian studies back up the Wellesley report with numbers. A 2002 Canadian study showed more women on a corporate board affecting the way a board performs and functions, with boards including two or more women assuming approximately twice the performance and accountability measures regularly. In six areas of good governance, diverse perspectives changed board processes. To learn more, review the report by David A.H. Brown, Debra L. Brown, and Vanessa Anastasopoulos, *Women on Boards: Not Just the Right Thing . . . The Bright Thing* (2002), available at www.europeanpwn.net/files/women_on_boards_canada.pdf.

Now more than ever, research demonstrates that representation of women or minorities on corporate boards may increase company profitability and improve board governance practices. Both contribute to shareholder value. A landmark 2007 Catalyst study found, when looking at return on equity, that Fortune 500 companies with three or more women board members outperformed those companies with the least women on the board by 53%.[212] Looking beyond the Fortune 500, an Oklahoma State University study published in 2002 found the same result in Fortune 1000 firms: a significant positive return on assets when compared with companies with a low number of women on the board.[213]

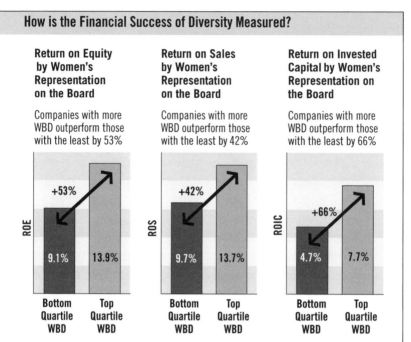

How is the Financial Success of Diversity Measured?

Return on Equity by Women's Representation on the Board

Companies with more WBD outperform those with the least by 53%

+53%
ROE
9.1% 13.9%

Bottom Quartile WBD | Top Quartile WBD

Return on Sales by Women's Representation on the Board

Companies with more WBD outperform those with the least by 42%

+42%
ROS
9.7% 13.7%

Bottom Quartile WBD | Top Quartile WBD

Return on Invested Capital by Women's Representation on the Board

Companies with more WBD outperform those with the least by 66%

+66%
ROIC
4.7% 7.7%

Bottom Quartile WBD | Top Quartile WBD

Key: ROE, ROS, and ROIC represent Return on Equity, Return on Sales, and Return on Invested Capital, respectively. WBD refers to women board directors.

Source: Catalyst, *The Bottom Line: Corporate Performance and Women's Representation on Boards* (2007). This report is the second in Catalyst's Business Case series, available at www.catalyst.org.

As mentioned earlier, the international community is implementing change. What will it take to increase boardroom gender diversity in the United States? To change the "look" of corporate boardrooms, we must dispel five key myths related to boardroom gender diversity:

Myth #1: Once one woman candidate has been added to a board, the work is done.

A company has done well to add one woman, but it has not added enough gender diversity to be effective. The *2010 Catalyst Census: Fortune 500 Women Board Directors* found only 20% of Fortune 500 boards have three or more women.[214] The numbers were much better—29.6% and

37.6%—when looking at boards with one or two women respectively. The onus is on all of us not only to encourage boards to diversify, but also to encourage them to continue to diversify after the first woman has been added. Only then will the overall percentages begin to resemble that 37.6% and will the women on boards begin to be heard.

How can you become an advocate for change? Everyone has some type of relationship with corporations —as an owner, investor, employee, or even a consumer of the company's products or services. Consider who is on those companies' boards of directors, and use your research and inquisitiveness to make the topic of boardroom diversity a priority. Start the conversation about gender diversity in the boardroom. Be an advocate for diversity in the boardroom.

Myth #2: The number of women on the board has nothing to do with the diversity of the rest of the company—nothing can be done.

Sitting women board members must take action in suggesting women candidates for CEO, senior management, and board roles. The number of women board directors is a proven predictor of the number of women in senior management. A lack of women on corporate boards means a lack of women in the room during recruitment and retention of the CEO and succession planning. Boards with a woman director compared to boards with no women directors showed a 45% increase in women in senior management over five years. Boards with two or more women directors, when compared to boards with a single woman director, had a 28% increase in women in senior management over five years.[215] A lack of a critical mass of women in the boardroom also results in a shortage of women as committee chairs, including Nominating Chair—a role many consider essential to true board power and useful in effectuating change.[216]

Similarly, companies with female CEOs tend to have more women directors. Each year, Spencer Stuart, a leading executive search firm, publishes an index of data about corporate governance. In 2010, this report found that the average percentage of women directors at companies with female CEOs is 32%. That same percentage at companies with male CEOs was only 15%.[217]

Although this might appear to be a "chicken-or-the-egg" conundrum—do women board members or women in senior management come first—research suggests that diversifying the corporate board is the way to start. Women board members must be passionate and encourage their boards to consider all resumes and utilize their networks to bring forward excellent candidates.

A plethora of research demonstrates that companies with diverse top management teams produce better corporate financial performance. For example, according to a Catalyst study, companies with gender diversity in upper management experience a nearly 35% greater return on equity and a 34% greater total return to shareholders than companies with no women in upper management.

Myth #3: The only candidate our board can ever consider is a sitting CEO, so we cannot locate any women candidates. There are very few sitting CEOs who are women.

False. More CEOs are limiting their outside board service to one company, so boards are more frequently looking beyond candidates with the title of sitting CEO.

One reason for the lack of gender diversity on boards may be the historical convention favoring a current or retired CEO for a board opening, due to that person's business experience. As most CEO positions have been occupied by non-minority men, this convention perpetuates the drive for the same candidates.

But these boards—still mostly men—no longer have the options they had in the past. The traditional candidate pool of sitting or former CEOs is now taxed to the limit.[218] "Twenty-six percent of this year's new directors are active CEOs, down from 53% a decade ago," finds Spencer Stuart, citing more functional leaders being recruited—closer to 18% of new board members are now functional leaders.[219] As mentioned above, there has been a "widespread redefinition of what constitutes a qualified [board] candidate," [220] a "seismic shift," leading companies to look towards new sources to fill director positions. Senior executives who previously had little chance of being invited to join a board are now in demand.[221] Board search experts report "a greater willingness by boards to consider candidates farther down in an organization . . . [including] senior functional or general management executives, including chief operating officers, chief information officers, CFOs and business unit leaders."[222]

Experience in areas such as information technology and finance are becoming increasingly attractive to boards searching for new candidates. The prevailing misperception of a lack of qualified senior executive women is a serious reason for the delay in achieving boardroom gender diversity. "Few Fortune 1000 CEOs are women . . . Boards must look beyond the obvious Fortune 1000 CEO candidate pool, [and] new processes must be established to identify highly qualified women with the skills to serve."[223] Considering candidates at additional executive levels immediately and significantly increases the pool of diversity candidates. For example, in the Fortune 500, women hold only 2.6% of CEO positions, but 14.6% of *corporate officer* positions. This creates a pool of 735 additional potential women board candidates.[224]

In the same survey, 44% of boards reported that they are looking to recruit women directors. However, only 21% of directors added in 2010 were women.[225] Why? One reason for the lack of gender diversity may be business leaders' natural instinct to surround themselves with others with whom they identify. Boards currently are mostly men, so it is their natural inclination to continue adding other men. Sitting board members and search consultants have reported many instances where women's resumes were being reviewed with a high level of scrutiny, until a male's resume comes along and is immediately accepted. If a board has changed its criteria, it should start over and try tapping the networks again. Boards should resist the temptation to select individuals whom board members know well. Though comforting, especially in tough economic times, is not always in the best interest of the company for positive group decision-making to include only directors with the same viewpoint.

A wide variety of organizations exist to help companies seeking women board members. These sources include:

- The Women Business Leaders of the U.S. Health Care Industry Foundation (WBL), a source of senior executive women candidates with experience in the health care industry. WBL assists with non-profit, for profit, public company, private company, and advisory searches. WBL serves as a source of supply and does not perform a screening function. As a result, WBL can work in conjunction with a search firm or internal search committee. See www.wbl.org for more.

- ION, a national alliance of fourteen prestigious women's business organizations located across the United States. ION's members share the mission of advancing women to positions of power in the business world, primarily to boards of directors and executive suites. ION is active in Atlanta, Dallas, Boston, Nashville, Kansas City, Chicago, New York, Northern California, Philadelphia, Detroit, Milwaukee, Minneapolis, Baltimore, and Florida. See www.ionwomen.org for information and links to ION's member sites.

- Women Corporate Directors, a powerful international organization comprised of women board members from around the world. To learn more, visit www.womencorporatedirectors.com.

- Boardroom Bound, a non-profit organization that works with companies to supply educated diversity candidates for board service. To learn more about Boardroom

Bound's board search and educational opportunities, visit www.boardroombound.biz.

■ The National Association of Corporate Directors, the trade association for corporate board members, maintains a Director's Registry of candidates that can be searched by gender or diversity metrics. See www.nacdonline.org to learn more.

■ The Women's Foodservice Forum, which maintains information on senior executive women candidates from the food and foodservice industries. For more information, visit www.womensfoodserviceforum.com.

Myth #4: Very few companies allow CEOs and senior executives to serve on outside boards.

Board service is an incredible way to gain exposure to new leadership topics. Indeed, 36% of those responding to Spencer Stuart's survey reported that they encourage internal CEO candidates to serve on outside public company boards as a means of gaining "broader leadership exposure." Presenting to any board is good experience, Spencer Stuart adds, saying that "[to] prepare top internal candidates for the CEO role, 94% [of boards] have them make presentations to the board."[226] Boards should consider allowing their executives to take advantage of the leadership opportunity offered by service on an outside board. Doing so not only would benefit the company tremendously, but also would help to create a larger pool of women candidates available to diversify corporate boardrooms. As mentioned earlier, 14.4% of corporate officer positions are held by women.[227] The chart that follows, **Limits on Outside Board Directorships,** outlines the extent to which S&P 500 boards allow CEOs and senior executives to serve on outside boards.

Limits on Outside Board Directorships

LIMITATION	CEOs	OTHER SENIOR EXECUTIVES
No outside board service permitted	4%	7%
1 outside board permitted	19%	17%
2 outside boards permitted	25%	9%
3 outside boards permitted	14%	7%
No limits on outside board service	38%	60%

Source: Spencer Stuart, *2010 Spencer Stuart Board Index*, page 15.

Should the board allow executives to serve on outside boards, executives must respond by being realistic about time to serve. Consider how your current employer will react to your interest in board service: Does it violate company policy? Does a company policy exist?

There are only twenty-four hours in a day. Be realistic about how much time you have to be a contributing member of a board, especially if your current employment is more than full time. The Spencer Stuart survey reported that only one third of senior management executives encouraged to serve on boards for leadership experience take advantage of the opportunity.[228]

The WBL Foundation publishes on its website a sample company policy to permit board service at an outside company. If your company has no written policy, consider using WBL's template to create such a policy. See www.wbl.org for details.

Myth #5: Women board members are the best mentors for women board candidates.

Not true—many WBL women have reported that their best mentors for board related opportunities have been male CEOs or male board members. Prospective board members can benefit from any relationship with board members. Board candidates should tell other executives and board members that they are interested in serving on a board of directors and ask those corporate insiders to make introductions to someone in their network. Maybe the CEO of your company is invited to join corporate boards frequently. Ask the CEO to refer some declined invitations to you, if appropriate. Network with current board members and board search consultants. Attend events to network with board members in a position to recommend candidates to other board members. If you meet board search consultants, schedule a private meeting to learn more about their practice, and for these consultants to learn more about you. If your company works with a search firm for executive placements, ask search firm representatives if their company also conducts board searches, and if you might be added to their database as someone with interest in board opportunities.

Women candidates should take advantage of opportunities to serve on international boards that are being mandated by foreign law to diversify. Do not discount smaller local companies or non-profit boards, which in some instances may be stepping stones that provide valuable experience and business networking opportunities. As the average age of boards has crept up since 1998 to 64 or older, opportunities will continue to knock.[229] Be prepared and be ready. WBL publishes a book with information about helping women in particular to be prepared. See www.wbl.org to order a copy of *Advancing Women in Business*.

Conclusion: Coming soon—A diversity "mandate" in the United States?

So why—if gender diversity is so good for shareholder value—would companies continue to have boards that are not more gender balanced? According to a survey by the National Association of Corporate Directors, 75% of boards do not have a plan in place to recruit more women and minorities.

Yet, over 50% of respondents to that survey believed they "should have such a plan."[230]

The Securities and Exchange Commission issued a rule in February 2010 (the 2010 Rules first mentioned in Chapter 3) requiring boards to disclose to the SEC "whether, and if so, how, a nominating committee considers diversity in identifying nominees for director." Boards that have existing diversity policies are required to disclose to the SEC how the policy is implemented and how its effectiveness is being evaluated.[231] This new federal regulatory guidance is the closest thing that the United States has in connection with board diversity regulatory initiatives. At this time, a diversity plan is not required for board recruitment.

Under this SEC rule, boards of public companies must provide information about "each director and director nominee," including "the particular experience, qualifications, attributes or skills that led the company's board to conclude that the person should serve as a director of the company." Significantly, the SEC does not define "diversity" so it may be interpreted simply as "diversity of experience."[232]

A number of other initiatives—some through states (Connecticut), some through investors (TIAA-CREF, CalPERS)—reference board diversity in their corporate governance guidelines as best practices.[233] Connecticut Treasurer Denise Nappier, chief fiduciary of the Connecticut Retirement Plans and Trust Funds, along with Calvert Group, Ltd., a private investor, have filed many shareholder resolutions relating to board diversity in order to encourage companies to seek diverse (in terms of both gender and ethnicity) candidates. Calvert Group, Ltd. "also created 'a model nominating committee charter for corporate boards as a means to institutionalize their commitment to a diverse and inclusive board,.' and has lobbied to have this language added to charters at major corporations." [234]

According to a 2010 report published by the ION organization, TK Kerstetter, CEO and President of Board Member, Inc., concluded that "[w]hat is required is a willingness—indeed an intentional effort—to look beyond the limited networks and resources traditionally used to populate corporate leadership, to recognize talent in whatever form it may take, and to build leadership teams that include at least several women and people of color." [235]

At current rates, studies estimate that it will take more than 70 years "for women to be equitably represented (50 percent) on boards." [236] There is no doubt that women are advancing—one by one—but a collision of factors are providing a true opportunity for boardroom gender diversity to increase in a meaningful way. Not only is research demonstrating that adding women to corporate boards is both practical and profitable, but boards are feeling a push, reflected in the best practices imposed or recommended by national governments, state governments, and large investment funds. As the SEC encourages boards to evolve and seek a more independent candidate list, there is a real opportunity to achieve a critical mass of senior executive women in U.S. for profit corporate boardrooms.

11 What Are Some Best Practices for Board Candidates and Board Members?

GUEST CHAPTER AUTHOR:
Jean Freeman, Jean Freeman & Associates

Much of this book is dedicated to finding a good match between you and a board of directors and being a compliant board member. Once you "Answer the Call," you will want to review the material in this book, especially Chapter Two, as well as other general resources. You will want to learn a number of things about the corporation and the board you have joined. Some companies have an orientation program for new board members. If there is no formal orientation, you should ask for a meeting with the board chair/president as soon as possible in order to gain an understanding about a number of key issues.

Due diligence questions

Of course, the corporation will be asking you questions as part of its due diligence to determine whether to extend an offer to you to be a new director. You also may want to pose questions to the corporation before accepting this director-ship. The following is a list of questions that, if you do not ask before accepting the position, you should consider asking once you are on the board.

- Why is there an opening on the board? Has there been a vacancy created by someone's leaving? Is the board expanding? Are there term limits for board members?

- What is the governance structure of this board? Are there standing committees or just ad hoc committees? Why? Do we use committees for limited purposes and disband them once the mission has been accomplished? How are committee appointments made? What are the expectations for individual board members to serve on committees?

- How often does the board meet? Where? What is the board's policy on payment of expenses?

- Has there been any significant litigation involving the corporation in the past few years? Is there any litigation pending?

- What protections are provided for me under our Directors and Officers liability coverage? (You may want to obtain a copy of the policy and have it reviewed by your own counsel. In addition, you may want to review the company's indemnification provisions in its articles and bylaws, and the applicable sections of the business corporation act of the state in which the company is incorporated. Chapter Four has additional questions to consider.)

- What are the duties of the board members as described in the bylaws, and what are the roles of the corporation's officers and committees?

- Is there legal counsel dedicated to the board's business? What is the role of the board's attorney?

- Who is the board's outside auditor? Have there been changes in the auditors over the past few years? Ask to see management letters from the outside auditors, if company policy does not prohibit it.

- What is the mission of the organization? (In addition to asking questions about the mission, goals, vision, etc., you may want to obtain a copy of the corporation's most recent strategic plan, financial statements, bylaws, and policies.)

- Does the corporation appear in the media? Does it actively participate in social media outlets? (There is a lot to learn from doing your own diligence on the internet about the corporation, existing directors, and management.)

■ In what ways does the board demonstrate transparency to its stakeholders (shareholders, members, customers, etc.)?

■ How long has the CEO been employed by the corporation? Have there been any significant turnovers in senior management or the board recently?

■ Does the corporation have a code of ethical conduct and a corporate compliance program? Is the code of ethical conduct displayed prominently in the office and on the website?

■ Does the corporate compliance program address industry-specific risks? If a corporation has a business arrangement with a government agency, such as the Medicare Program, a board member may want to make sure that the company's corporate compliance program includes adequate provisions specific to the risks of doing business with federal and state health care programs.[237]

What are some best practices to succeed as a director?

Once you are "on board," you will want to be the very best director you can be. There are many resources available today, including books and training programs to help you develop and improve your governance skills. You also will want to perform your duties according to accepted standards of good governance. The following is a list of best practices to consider:

(1) **Become comfortable speaking with your board chair, and ask questions, especially when you are a new board member.** If appropriate, identify and establish a relationship with a board member who can be your mentor. You may want to raise your questions to the board chair before and after meetings so that you can have more rapport and minimize your learning curve during board meetings.

(2) **Engage in the corporation and the industry**—with other board members, the CEO, other stakeholders.

(3) **Prepare for board meetings, committee meetings, and other corporate activities.** At a minimum, read all materials sent in advance of the meeting. Some boards are using online portals allowing board members access not only to necessary information, but also support materials for those desiring to explore an issue more fully.

(4) **Attend in person and participate in all board meetings.**

(5) **Vote.** Avoid the use of an abstention unless absolutely necessary. Vote only when you feel comfortable that you have answers to all of your questions.

(6) **Make decisions according to what is best for your organization**—not what is best for you or any other individual or group.

(7) **Avoid involvement in management issues.** Be clear about your governance role.

(8) **Encourage strategic thinking.** Help keep your board on track so that it is dealing with the over-arching issues appropriate to governance. Said one board member interviewed for this book, "If you do not like the way the meetings are playing out or the direction of the board's role, it is up to you to change it; do not be a witness."

(9) **Embrace transparency.** As you perform your duties as a board member, do so as if you are being observed by shareholders, stakeholders, etc.—even when you are not.

(10) **Disclose any potential conflict of interest.** If there is a potential conflict, raise it with your board chair to determine whether a conflict exists. If it is determined there is a conflict, remove yourself, not only from the vote, but also from the discussion.

(11) **Before taking on a board leadership position, understand the level of additional responsibility and prepare yourself for additional time commitments.** For instance, many board members have accepted the role of chair, incorrectly thinking it just meant running the meetings. Much responsibility comes with that job.

(12) **Encourage involvement in board self assessment/ evaluation.** Align your evaluation tools with your organization's strategic plan.

(13) **Be deliberate with your professional development as a board member.**

Best Practice: Board Evaluation

As mentioned earlier in this book, the NYSE requires listed corporations to conduct an evaluation of their own performance. Although it may not be a legal requirement for non-NYSE corporations, it is a best practice for a board of directors to have some type of self-evaluation process. The board and committee self-evaluation process should be viewed as a valuable tool to improve director, board, and corporate performance. The process should measure whether the board or committee effectively carried out the specific responsibilities assigned to it, as well as the more strategic aspects of board or committee performance.

For NYSE corporations, the nominating and corporate governance committee is responsible for overseeing board evaluations. For other boards, this likely would be the responsibility of the board chair. The evaluation process can be a very useful tool, especially if the topics evaluated focus on overall performance, rather than on individual board member performance.

There are numerous sample evaluation forms available, but the more closely the tool is tailored to a particular board, the more useful the outcomes can be. Some typical areas to evaluate include planning, monitoring of corporate and CEO performance, meeting effectiveness, mission and policy, financial support, and strategic focus. For example, the board member might be asked to assess these statements:

- The board's policy decisions reflect its mission.

- The board has established appropriate investment policies.

- The board considers all recommendations made in the independent auditor's report and management letter.

In addition to general areas such as these, a more useful evaluation could be tied directly to the corporation's strategic plan, assessing statements addressing that board's formal goals and strategies.

Resources for Professional Development

Management training is a part of many college curricula. In addition, most of us continue learning management principles at conferences, workshops, training programs, and through experience on the job. But very few of us have the opportunity to *study* governance. There are resources to do so. Many trade organizations provide director training. Some university programs address corporate governance. It is up to each board member to seek out opportunities to expand his or her professional development as a board member.

You may want to consider organizations such as the National Association of Corporate Directors (www.nacdonline.org) as resources once you are on a corporate board. This organization is dedicated to the professional development of board members and hosts a number of educational courses and forums for directors to engage. Other organizations, such as Women Corporate Directors (www.womencorporatedirectors.com) provide director education skills as well. You also may wish to consider subscribing to publications such as *Corporate Board Member* magazine or *Directors & Boards* magazine. Finally, WBL also offers sessions and webinars focusing on director-level skill sets, such as sessions where attendees can hear first-hand from sitting corporate directors.

Once on a corporate board, some directors choose to complete director education programs at schools such as Northwestern University's Kellogg Center for Executive Women, Stanford Graduate School of Business, or Wharton at the University of Pennsylvania.

Supporting women directors

For a number of reasons addressed in this book, there is increased scrutiny of the quality of board governance. As boards of directors are held more accountable, board diversity is closely watched as well. There are more women holding seats on both for profit and non-profit boards today than ever before but it is still a low number. As described in Chapter Ten, there is a significant value in having more women serving on boards. Consequently, leaders, both men and women, should be sure that boards are diverse and that diverse candidates can successfully contribute to the success of the board and the company as a whole. Consider the following excerpt from the Wellesley Centers for Women's 2006 Report:

- *Be sure that a woman's comments are heard; if the conversation goes on as though the woman has not spoken, reinforce what she has said and give her credit for it.*

- *If you notice a woman being ignored or slighted, let her know you see what is happening and then make it clear to others that you don't view this as acceptable board behavior.*

- *Be aware of informal occasions (golf for example) where women directors are not present and board business is discussed.*

- *Find time and ways to get to know the women informally to the same extent that you get to know the other men.*

- *Don't expect women to raise gender and diversity issues by themselves; be alert to those issues and take initiative to raise them also.*

- *Don't get suspicious that women are conspiring when women are seen talking or sitting together.*

- *Put women on nominating committees.*

- *Ask women, not only those on the nominating committee, to suggest women board candidates.*

- *Point out to the board that having one or two women is not enough.*

- *Insist that search firms and nominating committees provide diverse slates of board candidates.*[238]

Conclusion

Each board member should have the goal to serve the board and company with integrity, and with a commitment to perform responsibly. This requires professional development. This also requires a commitment to diversity and helping diverse candidates integrate within the board. This book is a resource to help you achieve this goal.

ABOUT THE PUBLISHER

 **Women Business Leaders of the U.S. Health Care Industry Foundation**™

The WBL Foundation is a non-profit organization founded in 2001 exclusively dedicated to senior executive women and women board members who work in or with the U.S. health care and life sciences industries. Unlike trade associations or other women's organizations, WBL provides a forum for these senior executive women and women board members in the health care industry to network exclusively with other senior executive women from across all segments of the health care industry. This includes manufacturers, payers, providers, and service providers to the health care industry. To date, more than 3,000 senior executive women and women board members participate in WBL. There are no dues. WBL's Foundation Associates participate by invitation only. WBL relies on an annual Summit and various sponsorships, educational forums, and publications, such as this book, in order to fund our year long activities.

All proceeds from this book benefit WBL. To learn more about the WBL Foundation, visit www.wbl.org.

WBL's Mission Statement

The mission of the WBL Foundation is to help senior executive women and women board members in the health care industry improve their businesses and continue to grow professionally. Our objectives to achieve that goal are to:

- facilitate networking opportunities for senior executive women and women board members in the health care industry;
- increase the visibility of senior executive women and women board members in the health care industry; and
- increase the number of senior executive women from the health care industry who serve as a member of a board of directors.

ABOUT THE AUTHORS

EPSTEINBECKERGREEN

About Epstein Becker & Green, P.C., founding sponsor of WBL

Founded in 1973, Epstein Becker & Green, P.C. (EBG) is a national law firm with a boutique approach to five complementary areas of practice. EBG's focus is on the core practice areas of:

- Business Law
- Health Care and Life Sciences
- Labor and Employment
- Litigation
- Real Estate

The firm has approximately 300 attorneys practicing in ten offices throughout the United States—Atlanta, Boston, Chicago, Houston, Los Angeles, New York, Newark, San Francisco, Stamford, and Washington D.C.—and law firm affiliates worldwide. EBG has one of the largest health care and life sciences law practices in the United States. The firm's website is located at www.ebglaw.com.

About the Authors

Lynn Shapiro Snyder, Esq. is a National Health Care & Life Sciences Practice Leader at Epstein Becker & Green, P.C., where she serves on the firm's Board and Finance Committees. She has been in EBG's Washington, D.C. office for over thirty-two years, advising clients about federal, state, and international health law issues, including Medicare, Medicaid, and managed care issues, as well as health care fraud defense and compliance. Her clients include health care and life sciences companies. Notably, she served as lead health counsel in many transactions including the HCA buyout, Biomet, and HCR ManorCare.

She has been recognized as one of the "Most Powerful People in Healthcare" and one of the best lawyers by various publications.

Ms. Snyder is the Founder, President, and Chair of the WBL Foundation, a non-profit organization comprised of more than 3,000 senior executive women and women board members worldwide who do business in the U.S. health care industry.

Ms. Snyder joined the board of Trustmark Companies in 2006. Trustmark provides life, medical, dental, managed care, wellness, disability, critical illness, accident insurance, and benefits administration services, with revenues over $1 billion. Trustmark recently purchased Health Fitness Corporation. She serves on the compensation and audit committees.

Ms. Snyder also is a board member of the Maryland/Israel Development Center, which encourages trade, joint ventures, and investment between Maryland and Israeli businesses and research institutions.

Ms. Snyder has authored two books about serving on corporate boards. She was named a "Director to Watch" by *Directors & Boards* magazine in August 2009.

Ms. Snyder can be reached at LSnyder@ebglaw.com.

Robert D. Reif is a member of the Epstein Becker & Green, P.C.'s Health Care and Life Sciences Practice in the firm's Washington, D.C. office and serves on the firm's Board of Directors. Additionally, he chairs the firm's National Business Law Practice, and heads the Corporate and Transactions subgroup in the Washington, D.C. office, specializing in all aspects of corporate and transactional law for the health care industry, including mergers and acquisitions and other financings, conversion of non-profit corporations to corporations for profit, obtaining state and federal certifications, provider contract negotiation and product development implementation.

Mr. Reif represents a variety of health care companies, including managed care organizations, hospitals, insurance and pharmaceutical companies, physician groups, managed mental health care companies, prepaid dental plan companies, preferred provider organizations, and utilization review companies.

Mr. Reif:

- Advises clients with regard to corporate structure, mergers and acquisitions, joint ventures, tax issues, including non-profit tax exemption matters, contracting, licensing requirements, risk management, and strategic planning;

- Serves as lead transaction counsel in a variety of health care company transactions aggregating over $1 billion in value;

- Advises companies, including venture capital companies, with regard to all aspects of the sales and acquisitions (non-hostile) of businesses;

- Counsels companies seeking outside financing, including negotiating venture capital transactions, bank and other debt-financing transactions, private placement of securities under state and federal securities laws, corporate reorganizations, and corporate conversions from non-profit to for profit status.

He holds a J.D. from Catholic University of America, Columbus School of Law and a B.A. from the University of Delaware.

He can be reached at rreif@ebglaw.com.

ABOUT THE CONTRIBUTING COMPANIES AND AUTHORS: CHAPTER FOUR

About Allied World Assurance Company

Allied World provides specialized solutions for the rapidly changing health care sector. Built upon a solid infrastructure of nearly three decades of health care experience, Allied offers a wide array of insurance products and solutions that address the unique and emerging exposures of this industry. Allied's industry-leading risk management services work to prevent losses before they occur, with experienced risk managers who understand the real risks and relevant issues. For more information, see www.awac.com.

About the Authors of Chapter Four

Susan R. Chmieleski, APRN, CPHRM, DFASHRM, JD, Senior Vice President, Global Risk Management and Loss Control Services, is responsible for the development of insurance products for healthcare-related business as well as risk management and loss control services in support of Allied World insurance offerings globally. She provides consulting and client services to policyholders, helping them assess and manage their organizational risk. Ms. Chmieleski has written numerous comprehensive education tools and brochures and is author to many published risk management articles. She is a regular presenter at the American Society of Healthcare Risk Management annual conference and faculty at PLUS University.

Ms. Chmieleski obtained a BS degree, summa cum laude, from the University of Hartford. She earned her JD degree from the University of Connecticut School Of Law, where she was editor-in-chief of the *Connecticut Insurance Law Journal*. Susan holds a Connecticut Nursing License and is an Advanced Practice Registered Nurse. She is a Certified Professional in Healthcare Risk Management, a former member of the Board of Directors and a Distinguished Fellow of the American Society for Healthcare Risk Management. She is licensed to practice law in Connecticut and is a member of the Connecticut and Hartford County Bar Associations.

Ms. Chmieleski can be reached at susan.chmieleski@awacservices.com.

see next page

Cynthia Oard, Senior Vice President, Practice Leader, Allied World Healthcare, is responsible for the management of the underwriting and operations of the health care division of Allied World Assurance Co. (U.S.). She has over twenty years of health care underwriting experience, joining Darwin Professional Underwriters in 2005 as Vice President of Health Care Underwriting. Her previous responsibilities have been for the strategy, products, distribution, and management of the Managed Care E&O and Health Care D&O books of business.

Prior to joining Darwin, Ms. Oard spent six years with Chubb, serving as both Chubb's Northern Zone and N.Y. Brokerage Zone Health Care Manager responsible for oversight of underwriting teams of Medical, Managed Care, and D&O production. Before its acquisition by Chubb, Ms. Oard spent twelve years with Executive Risk as their Midwest Regional Underwriting Manager and was an integral member of the team that developed the Executive Risk's entry into the managed care market.

Ms. Oard has been a featured speaker at numerous industry associations including the American Hospital Association and some of its state associations, PLUS, and the Health Care Financial Manager Association. Ms. Oard holds a Bachelor of Science from DePaul University. Ms. Oard can be reached at Cynthia.oard@awac.com.

ABOUT THE CONTRIBUTING COMPANIES AND AUTHOR: CHAPTER SEVEN

About Deloitte   **Deloitte.**

Deloitte refers to one or more of Deloitte Touch Tohmatsu Limited, a UK private company limited by guarantee, and its network of member firms, each of which is a legally separate and independent entity. Please see www.deloitte.com/about for a detailed description of the legal structure of Deloitte Touche Tohmatsu Limited and its member firms. Please see www.deloitte.com/about for a detailed description of the legal structure of Deloitte LLP and its subsidiaries. In the United States, Deloitte LLP and its subsidiaries have 45,000 professionals with a single focus: serving clients and helping them solve their toughest problems. Deloitte works in four key business areas — audit, financial advisory, tax and consulting. The Deloitte LLP Center for Corporate Governance offers a number of resources for executives, directors, and others who are active in governance, focusing on topics such as Audit Committees, Compensation Committees, Nominating/ Corporate Governance Committees, and Governance Reform.

Kimberly Zeoli is a national leader in Deloitte & Touche LLP's Health Sciences Regulatory and Compliance Advisory practice. She has twenty years of audit and consulting experience in health sciences serving over 100 public and private companies including health care providers, health plans and drug/device manufacturers. Her consulting career has focused on assisting clients and legal counsel with a variety of business risk issues. Recently, she served as an expert witness for public company on Medicare and commercial compliance matters.

Areas of specialization: governance, regulatory and risk strategies, enterprise risk management, corporate compliance programs, Medicare/Medicaid compliance, voluntary disclosures/settlements, audits/investigations, mergers and acquisitions, and financial relationships with health care providers.

Ms. Zeoli is a Certified Public Accountant licensed in California, New York and Massachusetts. She is an Advisory Board member of Women Business Leaders of the U.S. Health Care Industry Foundation (WBL), and Women Entrepreneurs in Science and Technology (WEST); and the co-leader of the Boston Chapter of Women Leaders in Health Sciences & Technology (Women Leaders). Ms. Zeoli is also a member of American Health Lawyers Association, the Society of Corporate Compliance and Ethics, and the Health Care Compliance Association.

In addition to her client service roles, Ms. Zeoli serves as the New England health sciences industry champion for her firm's women's initiative network called "WIN". Since Deloitte's WIN program was founded almost 20 years ago, the firm has received recognition and awards from many organizations for its dedication to women's advancement, diversity and inclusion, professional development and workplace flexibility. Over the years, Deloitte has been consistently ranked by Fortune, Business Week and Working Mother magazine among the best places to work.

Ms. Zeoli can be reached at kzeoli@deloitte.com.

ABOUT THE CONTRIBUTING COMPANIES AND AUTHOR: CHAPTER NINE

About K Fehling & Associates

K·Fehling
& Associates
People Define Companies

K Fehling & Associates is a retained search firm singularly focused within the life science industry, placing senior level executives in a broad range of clients from early-stage to Fortune 100 companies. Believing *People Define Companies*, KFA is known for its in-depth industry knowledge, focus and proven results. The company is headquartered in Jacksonville Beach, Florida with a west coast office in San Francisco, California. For more information, visit peopledefinecompanies.com.

About the Author or Chapter Nine

Kathleen H. Fehling, President of K. Fehling & Associates, became an executive search consultant in 2001, and founding K. Fehling & Associates, Inc. in 2003. Ms. Fehling has gained extensive experience fulfilling several President & CEO, CFO, COO and Corporate Director assignments, as well as numerous Vice President positions across all functional areas within the life science industry. Prior to becoming a search consultant, Ms. Fehling served as an officer of PSS World Medical, Inc. (NASDAQ:PSSI). During her time as the COO and CMO of the company's imaging subsidiary, Ms. Fehling led the integration of 46 acquisitions, growing the business from $70 million to $750 million in only three years. Previously, she served as a senior executive with Picker International (now part of Philips Medical Systems, Inc.). After graduating from Michigan State University with a pre-medical degree, Ms. Fehling began her career in sales with American Hospital Supply Corporation.

ABOUT THE CONTRIBUTING COMPANIES AND AUTHOR: CHAPTER TEN

About the WBL Foundation

See page 153 for more information.

About the Author or Chapter Ten

 **Eleanor Whitley** is the Executive Director of the Women Business Leaders of the U.S. Health Care Industry Foundation based in Washington, D.C. She is responsible for the successful planning, strategy, and execution of the organization's events, such as the annual Summit. She also is responsible for the organization's corporate governance-related initiatives, such as working with board search firms and other individuals to seek out corporate board opportunities for WBL's Foundation Associates. Ms. Whitley handles the general aspects of the Foundation's operation, such as the organization's financial statements and WBL publications.

Ms. Whitley joined the Foundation staff in 2004 as a Research Assistant. She holds a B.A. in Economics from the University of Virginia where she graduated with Honors.

ABOUT THE CONTRIBUTING COMPANIES AND AUTHOR: CHAPTER ELEVEN

About Jean Freeman & Associates

Jean Freeman & Associates was founded in 1992 in Washington, DC. This consulting firm provides services to help organizations become healthy, focused, and moving toward specific goals. Much of our work is in the area of governance. Our model, MACROgovernance,™ is easy to follow but helps keep boards on track, spending most of their time on the overarching duties of board members, not in the management trenches. Some of the services provided by Jean Freeman & Associates include:

- Strategic planning facilitation
- Training in management, governance, communication, leadership and customer service
- Developing board and organizational self-evaluation instruments
- Consulting with boards on governance or policy issues
- Organizational communication planning

The company website is www.jeanfreeman.com and its blog is www.jeanfreemanblog.com.

About the Author of Chapter Eleven

Since forming her company in 1992, **Jean Freeman** has been advising clients on issues of board governance, strategic planning, management leadership and organizational communication. The focus of her work is based on her model of governance, MACROgovernance.™ Boards following the principles of MACROgovernance keep their focus on the organization's mission and goals; satisfying their important fiduciary responsibilities. Jean advises clients on methods and practices which help Board members reach their overarching goals and help management steer the organizational ship on the course set by the Board/Management team in its strategic plan.

Jean Freeman has worked in the public and private sectors in fields such as health care and energy, with much of her consulting done with trade associations and other nonprofits. Since completing her Masters degree in Communication, she has gone on to complete the John Carver Policy Governance© Academy and to study industrial hygiene (worker health), employment and environmental law.

Her memberships include the Women Business Leaders of the U.S. Health Care Industry Foundation; American Management Association; International Association of Business Communicators; American Society of Association Executives; and she has served on the boards of Louisiana Safety Council; Governor's Highway Safety Commission; FGF, Inc.; and IHT, Inc. She regularly contributes articles on governance and management to a variety of publications, including her own blog at www.jeanfreemblog.com.

Endnotes

1   Spencer Stuart, *2010 Spencer Stuart Board Index*, 3 (2010).

2   National Association of Corporate Directors, *2009-2010 Director Compensation Survey*, 44 (Figure 19: Median Total Direct Compensation by Region and Company Size), available at www.nacdonline.org.

3   Russell Reynolds Associates, *2000-2001 Board Practices Survey, The Structure and Compensation of Boards of Directors of U.S. Public Companies,* 24 (2001).

4   Dorothy Light & Katie Pushor, *Into the Boardroom*, 4 (2002).

5   *See, e.g.*, Model Bus. Corp. Act, § 8.30(a) (2002 Supplement). State law determines specific requirements for board members.

6   *See, e.g.*, Model Nonprofit Corp. Act, § 8.30(a) (1987). State law determines specific requirements for board members.

7   *See, e.g.*, Model Bus. Corp. Act, §§ 8.30(d) and 8.30(e) (2002 Supplement). State law determines specific requirements for board members.

8   *Id.*

9   Gantler v. Stephens, 965 A.2d 695, 709 (Del. 2009); see also McPadden v. Sidhu, 964 A.2d 1262, 1275 (Del. Ch. 2008) (citing Ryan v. Gifford, 935 A.2d 258, 269 (Del. Ch. 2007) (citing In re Walt Disney Co., No. 15452, 2004 WL 2050138, at *3 (Del. Ch. Sept. 10, 2004)) ("The fiduciary duties an officer owes to the corporation 'have been assumed to be identical to those of directors.'").

10 *See, e.g.*, Oliver v. Boston Univ., 2006 Del. Ch. LEXIS 75 (Del. Ch. 2006), *aff'd*, 2009 Del. Ch. LEXIS 96 (Del. Ch. 2009) (clarifying fees and payments under the prior judgment).

11 *See generally* United States Department of Health and Human Services, Office of Inspector General & American Health Lawyers Association, *Corporate Responsibility and Corporate Compliance: A Resource for Health Care Boards of Directors* (2003); United States Department of Health and Human Services, Office of Inspector General & American Health Lawyers Association, *An Integrated Approach to Corporate Compliance: A Resource for Health Care Organization Boards of Directors (Supplement to 2003 Publication)* (July 1, 2004).

[12] Andrea Bonime-Blanc & Jacqueline Brevard, The Conference Board, *Ethics & the Board: Integrating Integrity into Business Strategy* (December 2009), available at www.conference-board.org/publications/publicationdetail.cfm?publicationid=1789.

[13] *Id.* at 15.

[14] *See id.* at 15-19.

[15] Bernard Black, Brian Cheffins & Michael Klausner, Outside Director Liability, *Stanford Law Review*, 1055 (February 2006).

[16] Fletcher Cyc. Corp., § 1041.10, 54. *See also* Stepak v. Addison, 20 F.3d 398 (11th Cir. 1994).

[17] Emily A. Moseley & Hayden J. Silver, III, *Building a Strong Board of Directors/Advisors & Board Best Practices Primer*, under Personal Liability of Board Members, 3 (2001).

[18] Fletcher Cyc. Corp., 55. *See also* Stepak v. Addison, 20 F.3d 398 (11th Cir. 1994).

[19] Fletcher Cyc. Corp., 58. *See also* Model Business Corporation Act (1984).

[20] Moseley & Silver, *supra* note 17.

[21] Paula Desio, *An Overview of the United States Sentencing Commission and the Organizational Guidelines*, available at www.ussc.gov/Guidelines/Organizational_Guidelines/ORGOVERVIEW.pdf (last visited Feb.12, 2011).

[22] Caremark International Inc. Derivative Litigation, 698 A. 2d 959 (Del.Ch. 1996).

[23] *Id.* at 970.

[24] *Id.* at 969.

[25] *Id.* at 969-970.

[26] *Id.* at 971.

[27] Richard De Rose, Fiduciary Duties in Turbulent Times, *NACD Directorship*, Vol. 36, No.1, 46-47 (Feb.-Mar. 2010).

[28] *Id.* at 47.

[29] *Id. See In re* Citigroup Inc. Shareholder Derivative Litigation, 964 A.2d 106 (Del. Ch. 2009).

[30] *In re* The Walt Disney Co. Deriv. Litig., 906 A.2d 27 (Del. 2006).

[31] *Id.* at 67.

[32] The Securities and Exchange Commission, *About the SEC, The Laws That Govern the Securities Industry*, available at www.sec.gov/about/laws.shtml (last visited Feb. 7, 2011).

[33] *Id.*

[34] *Id.*

[35] Moseley & Silver, *supra* note 17, 1.

[36] Louis Lavelle, The Best and Worst Boards, How the Corporate Scandals are Sparking a Revolution in Governance, *BusinessWeek* (October 7, 2002), available at www.businessweek.com.

[37] Fletcher Cyc. Corp., § 900.15, 402, note 1. *See also* Reliance Elec. Co. v. Emerson Elec., 404 U.S. 418 (1972).

[38] Pub. L. No. 107-204, 116 Stat. 745. 15 U.S.C. 78p(a)(2)(C).

[39] Moseley & Silver, *supra* note 17.

[40] Fletcher Cyc. Corp., §1344.10, 562. *See also* King v. Gibbs, 876 F.2d 1275 (7th Cir. 1989).

[41] Moseley & Silver, *supra* note 17, 2.

[42] Pub. L. No. 111-203, 124 Stat. 1376.

[43] *Id.*

[44] Phil Mattingly and Patrick O'Connor, *Financial Overhaul is Law, Now Comes Battle Over its Rules*, Bloomberg (July 21, 2010), available at www.bloomberg.com/news/2010-07-21/obama-signs-biggest-overhaul-of-financial-rules-since-the-great-depression.html.

[45] *See* Chairman Mary L. Schapiro, *Testimony Concerning Oversight of the U.S. Securities and Exchange Commission: Evaluating Present Reforms and Future Challenges* (July 20, 2010), available at www.sec.gov/news/testimony/2010/ts072010mls.htm.

[46]   Joe Masterson, Dodd-Frank Act Could Be A Home Run (Sept. 9, 2010), available at www.biztimes.com/news/2010/ 9/3/dodd-frank-act-could-be-a-home-run.

[47]   United States Senate Committee on Banking, Housing, & Urban Affairs, *Brief Summary Of The Dodd-Frank Wall Street Reform And Consumer Protection Act,* (July 1, 2010) available at http://banking. senate.gov/public/_files/070110_Dodd_Frank_Wall_Street_Reform_ comprehensive_summary_Final.pdf.

[48]   Pub. L. No. 111-203 § 971, 124 Stat. 1376.

[49]   SEC Press Release, *SEC Approves Enhanced Disclosure About Risk, Compensation and Corporate Governance* (Dec. 16, 2009), available at www.sec.gov/news/press/2009/2009-268.htm (hereinafter *SEC Press Release 2009*).

[50]   *Id.*

[51]   74 Fed. Reg. 68334 (Dec. 23, 2009).

[52]   *SEC Press Release 2009.*

[53]   74 Fed. Reg. 68337 (Dec. 23, 2009).

[54]   Pub. L. No. 111-203 at § 951.

[55]   *Id.* at § 953.

[56]   Pub. L. No. 111-203, 124 Stat. 1376.

[57]   United States Senate Committee on Banking, Housing, & Urban Affairs, *Brief Summary Of The Dodd-Frank Wall Street Reform And Consumer Protection Act,* (July 1, 2010) available at http://banking. senate.gov/public/_files/070110_Dodd_Frank_Wall_Street_Reform_ comprehensive_summary_Final.pdf.

[58]   *SEC Press Release 2009.*

[59]   74 Fed. Reg. 68345 (Dec. 23, 2009).

[60]   Pub. L. No. 111-203 § 972.

[61]   17 CFR § 229.401 (3) *as amended by* 74 Fed. Reg. 68334 (Dec 23, 2009).

[62]   *Id.*

[63]   Fletcher Cyc. Corp., § 5432, 58. *See also* EBS Litigation LLC v. Barclays Global Investors, N.A., 304 F.3d 302 (3d Cir. 2002).

[64] Fletcher Cyc. Corp., 59. *See also* Aiken v. Insull, 122 F.2d 746 (7th Cir. 1941), *cert. den.* 315 U.S. 806 (1942).

[65] 33 U.S.C. § 1251 et seq. (2000).

[66] The Comprehensive Environmental Response, Compensation, and Liability Act (CERCLA), also known as Superfund, involves treatment and release of hazardous waste. *See* www.epa.gov/superfund/policy/cercla.htm for more information.

[67] Fletcher Cyc. Corp., § 1234.24, 343, note 4. *See also* United States v. USX Corp., 68 F3d 811 (3d Cir. 1995).

[68] Fletcher Cyc. Corp., § 1264, 369, note 2. *See also* Vinick v. C.I.R., 110 F.3d 168 (1st Cir. 1997).

[69] I.R.C. § 4958; Treas. Reg. § 53.4958-6.

[70] Pub. L. No. 111-5 (2009).

[71] 45 C.F.R. § 160.103.

[72] For the definition of "protected health information," see 45 C.F.R. § 164.501.

[73] Pub. L. No. 111-5 (2009).

[74] 29 U.S.C. § 1001 *et seq.* (2000).

[75] U.S. Department of Labor, *Employee Retirement Income Security Act—ERISA*, available at www.dol.gov/dol/topic/health-plans/erisa.htm (last visited Feb. 7, 2011).

[76] Fletcher Cyc. Corp., § 6753, 325, note 4. *See also* 29 U.S.C. § 1002 (21).

[77] *Id.* at 326. *See also* 29 U.S.C. § 1109 (21).

[78] *See* 15 U.S.C. §§ 78dd-1, *et seq.* Under the anti-bribery provisions of the FCPA, it is unlawful for a U.S. person, U.S. company, or any other person in the U.S. with corrupt intent to offer, pay, promise to pay, or authorize payment of, directly or indirectly, anything of value to a foreign official, foreign political party, any candidate for foreign political office, or any other person while knowing that all or a portion of the payment will be offered, given, or promised, directly or indirectly, to a covered person for the purpose of influencing any official act or decision, inducing any act or omission in violation of a lawful official duty, or securing an improper advantage in order to assist in obtaining, retaining, or directing business to any person.

[79] *See* 15 U.S.C. § 78m. The accounting provisions subject an issuer to recordkeeping and disclosure requirements and mandate that issuers adopt internal accounting controls. Under the FCPA, issuers are required to make and keep books, records, and accounts which, in reasonable detail, accurately and fairly reflect the transactions and dispositions of the assets of the issuer; and devise and maintain a system of internal accounting controls sufficient to provide reasonable assurance that transactions are properly authorized, recorded, and audited.

[80] Entities that violate the anti-bribery provisions face a maximum fine of $2 million per violation, and individuals face a maximum fine of $100,000 and 5 years imprisonment per violation. Alternatively, the federal government can seek fines of $500,000 for entities and $250,000 for individuals, or double the gross gain or loss from the unlawful activity. For violations of FCPA accounting provisions, the SEC can impose the same civil remedies and penalties available under the SEC's general enforcement authority. For falsifying books and records or knowingly circumventing—or failing to implement—internal controls, companies can face fines of $25 million and individuals can face fines of $5 million and 20 years imprisonment.

[81] John R. Engen, What Are Your Chances of Going to Jail?, *Corporate Board Member*, Special Legal Issue (2002).

[82] *Id.* at 1.

[83] *Id.* at 1.

[84] Kevin M. Lacroix, Outside Director Exposure for Disclosure Violations, *The D&O Diary* (Apr. 9, 2010), available at www.dandodiary.com/2010/04/articles/outside-director-liability/outside-director-exposure-for-disclosure-violations/.

[85] SEC Press Release, *SEC Charges Former Executives in Illegal Scheme to Enrich CEO with Perks* (Mar. 15, 2010), available at www.sec.gov/news/press/2010/2010-39.htm.

[86] *SEC v. Raval*, Complaint at 1 (D. Neb. March 15, 2010), available at www.sec.gov/litigation/complaints/2010/comp21451-raval.pdf.

[87] Engen, *supra* note 81 at 2.

[88] *Id.*

[89] Ernst & Young, *SEC in Focus: Quarterly Summary of Current SEC Activities*, Issue 1 (Jan. 2010), available at www.ey.com/Global/assets.nsf/United%20Accounting/ATG_SEC_CC0292/$file/ATG_SEC_CC0292.pdf (hereinafter *SEC in Focus Issue 1*).

90 *Id.*

91 Stephen Barlas, Obama Administration establishes corporate fraud task force, *Strategic Finance* (Jan. 1, 2010), available at www.allbusiness.com/legal/legal-services-litigation/13757350-1.html.

92 *Id.*

93 *Id.*

94 *SEC in Focus Issue 1.*

95 Greg Morcroft, Holder details focus of financial-fraud task force, *MarketWatch* (Jan. 8, 2010), available at www.marketwatch.com/story/holder-details-focus-of-financial-fraud-task-force-2010-01-08 (hereinafter *Holder details*).

96 The Recovery Act was passed in early 2009 as a direct response to the financial crisis of 2008. The Recovery Act distributed funds nationwide with the stated goals of creating new jobs, spurring economic activity, and enhancing transparency in government spending. For more information on the Recovery Act and its application, see the U.S. government's official website at www.recovery.gov

97 *Holder details.*

98 Black, Cheffins & Klausner, *supra* note 15.

99 *Id.*

100 *Id.* at 1056 (emphasis added).

101 Eds. David B. Nash, William J. Oetgen & Valerie P. Pracilo, *Governance for Health Care Providers: The Call to Leadership* (2009), 161 (hereinafter *Governance for Health Care Providers*).

102 *Id.*

103 *Id.*

104 Anthony S. Chan, *Manager's Guide to Compliance: Sarbanes-Oxley, COSO, ERM, COBIT, IFRS, BASEL II, OMB's A-123, ASX 10, OECD Principles, Turnbull Guidance, Best Practices, and Case Studies,* The CPA Journal (Oct. 1, 2006), available at www.allbusiness.com/finance/business-insurance-risk-management/4094580-1.html.

[105] *Governance for Health Care Providers, supra* note 105 at 162 (citing Committee of Sponsoring Organizations of the Treadway Commission, *Enterprise Risk Management—Integrated framework—Executive Summary* (Sep. 2004), available at www.coso.org/Publications/ERM/COSO_ERM_ ExecutiveSummary.pdf.) The Committee of Sponsoring Organizations of the Treadway Commission (COSO) is a voluntary private-sector organization, established in the United States, dedicated to providing guidance to executive management and governance entities on critical aspects of organizational governance, business ethics, internal control, enterprise risk management, fraud, and financial reporting. COSO has established a common internal control model against which companies and organizations may assess their control systems.

[106] *Id.*

[107] Committee of Sponsoring Organizations of the Treadway Commission, *Enterprise Risk Management—Integrated framework— Executive Summary*, 3 (Sep. 2004), available at www.coso.org/Publications/ERM/COSO_ERM_ExecutiveSummary.pdf.

[108] Engen, *supra* note 81.

[109] Black, Cheffins & Klausner, *supra* note 15, 1056.

[110] Stewart M. Landefeld, Andrew B. Moore & Katherine Ann Ludwig, Eds., *The Public Company Handbook, A Practical Guide for Directors and Executives*, 120 (May 2002).

[111] *Id.*

[112] David M. Gische & Vicki E. Fishman, Ross Dixon & Bell, LLP, Directors and Officers Insurance Liability, 1 (2000).

[113] *Id.* at 2.

[114] *Id.* at 2.

[115] Towers Watson, *Directors and Officers Liability Survey* —2010 Summary of Results, available at http://www.towerswatson.com/assets/pdf/3790/DandO_Survey_2011.pdf (last visited Feb. 7, 2011).

[116] Gerald Griffith, Michael Peregrine, Ralph DeJong, Paul DeMuro, Daniel Hale, David Hillman, Louise Joy, Shannon Kelley, John Libby, Gerald McGovern, Cynthia Reaves, & James Schwartz, Esqs. *Lessons for Healthcare from Enron: A Best Practices Handbook*, 149 (2002).

[117] John E. Black, Jr. & David T. Burrowes. IRMI, *D&O Litigation Trends in 2006* (May 2007); IRMI, *D&O Litigation Trends in 2007* (May 2007).

[118] Towers Watson, *supra* note 115.

[119] *Id.* at 5.

[120] Gische & Fishman, *supra* note 112.

[121] *Id.*

[122] Moseley & Silver, *supra* note 17 at 2.

[123] Gische & Fishman, *supra* note 112 at 8.

[124] *Id.*

[125] Pub. L. No. 107-204, 116 Stat. 745. 15 U.S.C. § 7241 (Section 302) (Civil); 18 U.S.C. § 1350 (Section 906) (criminal provision).

[126] Amy Borrus, *Learning to Love Sarbanes-Oxley,* BusinessWeek 126 (Nov. 21, 2005).

[127] Angie Mohr, *The Sarbanes-Oxley Act Eight Years Later* (June 28, 2010), available at www.associatedcontent.com/article/5519474/ the_sarbanesoxley_act_eight_years_later.html.

[128] Management's Report on Internal Control over Financial Reporting and Certifications of Disclosure in Exchange Act Periodic Reports, Final Rule, Securities Release No. 8392, Exchange Act Release No. 49,313 (Feb. 4, 2004), 69 Fed. Reg. 9722 (March 1, 2004).

[129] *Free Enterprise Fund v. Public Company Accounting Oversight Board,* No. 08-861 (U.S., June 28, 2010).

[130] *Id.*

[131] These rules became effective on August 5, 2003. Implementation of Standards of Professional Conduct for Attorneys, Securities Release No. 8185, Exchange Act Release No. 47,276 (Jan. 29, 2003), 68 Fed. Reg. 6296 (Feb. 6, 2003).

[132] Certifications of Disclosure in Companies' Quarterly and Annual Reports, Securities Release No. 33-8124, Exchange Act Release No. 46,427 (Aug. 29, 2002), 67 Fed. Reg. 57276 (Sept. 9, 2002).

[133] 15 U.S.C. § 78p (2007) (requiring directors, officers, and principal stockholders to file statements with the SEC).

134   Item 406, Regulation S-K, 17 C.F.R. § 229.406 (2003). *See also* Disclosure Required by Sections 406 and 407 of the Sarbanes-Oxley Act of 2002, Securities Release No. 8177, Exchange Act Release No. 47,235 (Jan. 23, 2003), 68 Fed. Reg. 5110 (Jan. 31, 2003), *subsequent correction in* Securities Release No. 8177A, Exchange Act Release No. 47,325A (Mar. 26, 2003), 68 Fed. Reg. 15353 (Mar. 31, 2003).

135   Disclosure Required by Sections 406 and 407 of the Sarbanes-Oxley Act of 2002, Securities Release No. 8177, Exchange Act Release No. 47,235 (Jan. 23, 2003), 68 Fed. Reg. 5110. *See also* Item 5.05 of Form 8-K, 17 C.F.R. § 249.308 (2003).

136   Sarbanes-Oxley Act § 806, 18 U.S.C. § 1514A (2002).

137   United States Senate Committee on Banking, Housing, & Urban Affairs, *Brief Summary Of The Dodd-Frank Wall Street Reform And Consumer Protection Act,* available at http://banking.senate.gov/public/_files/070110_Dodd_Frank_Wall_Street_Reform_comprehensive_summary_Final.pdf. (July 1, 2010).

138   Weil, Gotshal & Manges, *Financial Regulatory Reform: An Overview of The Dodd-Frank Wall Street Reform and Consumer Protection Act,* available at www.weil.com/files/upload/Weil%20Dodd-Frank%20Overview.pdf (last visited Feb. 7, 2011).

139   Public Company Accounting Oversight Board, Order Approving Proposed Auditing Standard No. 2, *An Audit of Internal Control Over Financial Reporting Performed in Conjunction with an Audit of Financial Statements,* Exchange Act Release No. 49,884 (June 17, 2004), 69 Fed. Reg. 35083 (providing professional standards and guidance for independent auditors to attest to managements' reports on internal controls over financial reporting).

140   GAO, *Report to the Committee on Small Business and Entrepreneurship, U.S. Senate, Sarbanes-Oxley Act: Consideration of Key Principles Needed in Addressing Implementation for Smaller Public Companies,* at 17 (Apr. 2006), available at www.gao.gov/new.items/d06361.pdf.

141   Amendments to Rules Regarding Management's Report on Internal Control Over Financial Reporting, Securities Release No. 33-8809, Exchange Act Release No. 55,928 (June 20, 2007), 72 Fed. Reg. 35310 (June 27, 2007).

142   Pub L. No. 111-203, 125 Stat. 1376.

143   *Id.*

[144] *See* Final Rule: Additional Form 8-K Disclosure Requirements and Acceleration of Filing Date, Securities Release No. 8400, Exchange Act Release No. 49,424 (Mar. 25, 2004), 69 Fed. Reg. 15593 (March 25, 2004), *subsequent correction in* Securities Release No. 8400A, Exchange Act Release No. 49,424A (Aug. 4, 2004), 69 Fed. Reg. 48370 (Aug. 10, 2004).

[145] *Id.*

[146] 18 U.S.C. § 1513(e) (2002) (amending the obstruction of justice statute to include a prohibition against retaliation).

[147] Implementation of Standards of Professional Conduct for Attorneys, Securities Release No. 8185, Exchange Act Release No. 47,276 (Jan. 29, 2003).

[148] American Institute of Certified Public Accountants, *The State Cascade— An Overview of the State Issues Related to the Sarbanes-Oxley Act,* available at www.aicpa.org (last visited Feb. 7, 2011).

[149] *See generally* NYSE Euronext, *American Stock Exchange Historical Timeline,* available at www.nyse.com/pdfs/AmexTimeline.pdf (last visited Feb. 26, 2011).

[150] *See* www.nyse.com/about/history/1089312755484.html (last visited Feb. 26, 2011).

[151] On March 7, 2006, the NYSE became a for profit corporation. *See* www.nyse.com/about/history/1022221392987.html (last visited Feb. 26, 2011).

[152] The listings directory is online at www.nyse.com/about/listed/ 1089312755443.html (last visited Feb. 26, 2011).

[153] The transaction is subject to regulatory approval in Europe and the United States. Shira Ovide, NYSE-Deutsche Borse Merger: The Full Statement, *Wall Street Journal* (Feb. 9, 2011), available at http://blogs.wsj.com/deals/2011/02/09/nyse-deutsche-borse-merger-the-full-statement/.

[154] NASDAQ Press Release, *Nasdaq Marks 30th Anniversary* (Feb. 8, 2001), available at www.nasdaq.com/Newsroom/news/pr2001/ne_section01_040.html.

[155] *See* www.nasdaq.com/about/overview.stm (last visited Feb. 26, 2011).

[156] Self Regulatory Organizations; New York Stock Exchange, Inc. and National Association of Securities Dealers, Inc.; Order Approving Proposed Rule Changes (SR-NYSE-2002-33 and SR-NASD-2002-141) and Amendments No. 1 Thereto; Order Approving Proposed Rule Changes (SR-NASD-2002-77, SR-NASD-2002-80, SR-NASD-2002-138 and SR-NASD-2002-139) and Amendments No. 1 to SR-NASD-2002-80 and SR-NASD-2002-139; and Notice of Filing and Order Granting Accelerated Approval of Amendment Nos. 2 and 3 to SR-NYSE-2002-33, Amendment Nos. 2,3,4 and 5 to SR-NASD-2002-141, Amendment Nos. 2 and 3 to SR-NASD-2002-80, Amendment Nos. 1, 2, and 3 to SR-NASD-2002-138, and Amendment No. 2 to SR-NASD-2002-139, Relating to Corporate Governance, 68 Fed. Reg. 64154 (Nov. 12, 2003).

[157] SEC Commissioner Cynthia Glassman, Remarks before the 2005 Colloquium for Women Directors, Board Diversity: The 21st Century Challenge: The New Regulatory Climate and Impact on Board Composition (Nov, 11, 2005, New York, New York), available at www.sec.gov/news/speech/spch111105cag.htm.

[158] Certain deferrals and exemptions apply to certain types of companies and in connection with certain transactions such as an Initial Public Offering (IPO).

[159] *General Commentary to Section 303A.02(b) of the NYSE Listed Company Manual. http://phx.corporate-ir.net/External.File?item=UG-FyZW50SUQ9NTA5MTJ8Q2hpbGRJRD0tMXxUeXBlPTM=&t=1*

[160] Section 303A Corporate Governance Rules (as of Nov. 3, 2004), available at www.nyse.com/pdfs/section303A_final_rules.pdf; NYSE Listed Company Manual Section 303A Corporate Governance Listing Standards Frequently Asked Questions (updated as of Feb.13, 2004), available at www.nyse.com/pdfs/section303Afaqs.pdf.

[161] NASDAQ, Corporate Governance Rules 5600 and Associate Interpretative Material (Apr. 15, 2004 and as amended Mar. 12, Apr. 27, May 20, June 16, Aug. 18, 2009, Mar. 15, May 14, and July 22, 2010), *see* www.nasdaq.com/about/RegRequirements.pdf; NASDAQ, Frequently Asked Questions, Corporate Governance Rules & The Interpretive Process, available at www.nasdaq.com/about/FAQsCorpGov.stm (last visited Feb. 26, 2011).

[162] Section 303A Corporate Governance Rules (as of Nov. 3, 2004), available at www.nyse.com/pdfs/section303A_final_rules.pdf.

[163] NASDAQ, Corporate Governance Rules 4200, 4350, 4351, and 4360 and Associate Interpretative Material (Apr. 15, 2004) available at www.nasdaq.com/about/CorporateGovernance.pdf.

[164]   Jeffrey N. Gordon, The Rise of Independent Directors in the United States, 1950-2005: Of Shareholder Value and Stock Market Prices, 59 *Stan. L. Rev.* 1465, 1472-76 (2007).

[165]   Spencer Stuart US Board Index 2010 (Oct. 2010), available at www.spencerstuart.com/research/articles/1454/ (based on an analysis of the proxy statements from 491 companies filed between May 15, 2009 and May 15, 2010, and responses from 92 companies to governance survey conducted in the second quarter of 2010).

[166]   *See* Report of the Task Force of the ABA Section of Business Law Corporate Governance Committee 15 (Aug. 18, 2009) (hereinafter *ABA Report*); *see also* The Aspen Institute, *Overcoming Short-termism: A Call for a More Responsible Approach to Investment and Business Management* 2 (Sept. 9, 2009), available at www.aspeninstitute.org/ sites/default/files/content/docs/pubs/overcome_short_state0909_0.pdf; The Aspen Institute, Long-Term Valuation Creation: Guiding Principles for Corporations and Investors (June 2007), available at www.aspeninstitute.org/sites/default/files/content/docs/pubs/Aspen_ Principles_with_signers_April_09.pdf.

[167]   *See generally* John Laide, *Shareholder Activism Continues to Increase While Takeover Defenses Decline* (Jan. 7, 2008), available at www.sharkrepellent.net/request?an=dt.getPage&st=1&pg=/pub/rs_200 80107.html&rnd=133234; John Laide, *Trend Toward Removing Takeover Defenses Continues* (Jan. 17, 2006), available at www.sharkrepellent.net/request?an=dt.getPage&st=1&pg=/pub/rs_200 60117.html&rnd=808576. *See ABA Report,* supra note 166 at 13-14.

[168]   Gordon, Jeffrey N., The Rise of Independent Directors in the United States, 1950-2005: Of Shareholder Value and Stock Market Prices, 59 *Stan. L. Rev.* 1465, 1472-76 (2007).

[169]   For NYSE programs, see www.boardmember.com/education.aspx and for NASDAQ programs see www.nacdonline.org/NASDAQ.

[170]   *See generally* The Institute of Internal Auditors at www.theiia.org.

[171]   SEC, *New Shareholder Voting Rules for the 2010 Proxy Season,* available at www.sec.gov/investor/alerts/votingrules2010.htm (last visited Feb. 7, 2011).

[172]   SEC, 17 C.F.R. Parts 228, 229 and 249, Disclosure Required by Sections 406 and 407 of the Sarbanes-Oxley Act of 2002, available at www.sec.gov/rules/final/33-8177.htm (last visited April 22, 2011).

[173]   *Id.*

[174]   *Id.*

[175]   Thomas E. Wilson, Females and Financial Experts: Board Diversity in the Era of the SEC's Audit Committee Requirements, *Academy of Accounting and Financial Studies Journal* (Oct. 1, 2010), available at www.faqs.org/periodicals/201010/2122340271.html.

[176]   U.S. Sentencing Commission, *Federal Sentencing Guidelines Manuals,* available at www.ussc.gov.

[177]   Paula Desio, Deputy General Counsel, United States Sentencing Commission, *An Overview of the Organizational Guidelines,* available at www.ussc.gov/Guidelines/Organizational_Guidelines/ ORGOVERVIEW.pdf (last visited April 22, 2011).

[178]   U.S. Sentencing Commission, *Chapter 8 Organizational Guidelines,* available at www.ussc.gov/Guidelines/Organizational_Guidelines/ guidelines_chapter_8.htm (effective November 1, 2010) (last visited April 22, 2011).

[179]   U.S. Department of Justice, Office of the Deputy Attorney General, *Memorandum from Paul J. McNulty, Federal Prosecution of Business Organizations*, Revised Principles (Dec. 2006).

[180]   2010 Federal Sentencing Guidelines Manual, Chapter Eight Sentencing of Organizations, available at www.ussc.gov/Guidelines/2010_ guidelines/ Manual_HTML/8b2_1.htm (last visited April 22, 2011).

[181]   The three documents co-sponsored by the Office of Inspector General of the U.S. Department of Health and Human Services and The American Health Lawyers Association are: *Corporate Responsibility and Corporate Compliance: A Resource for Health Care Boards of Directors* (2003); *An Integrated Approach to Corporate Compliance: A Resource for Health Care Organization Boards of Directors* (2004); and *Corporate Responsibility and Health Care Quality: A Resource for Health Care Boards of Directors* (2007).

[182]   Deloitte, *Audit Committee Resource Guide,* available at www.corpgov.deloitte.com (last visited Feb. 7, 2011).

[183]   Deloitte refers to one or more of Deloitte Touche Tohmatsu Limited, a UK private company limited by guarantee, and its network of member firms, each of which is a legally separate and independent entity. Please see www.deloitte.com/about for a detailed description of the legal structure of Deloitte Touche Tohmatsu Limited and its member firms. Please see www.deloitte.com/us/about for a detailed description of the legal structure of Deloitte LLP and its subsidiaries.

[184] James J. Fishman, Standards of Conduct for Directors of Non-profit Corporations, 7 *Pace Law Rev.* 389, 442 (1987).

[185] IRC § 501(c)(3); Treas. Reg. § 1.501(a)-1(c) and §1.501(c)(3)-1.

[186] Internal Revenue Service, *Sample Conflicts of Interest Policy*, Appendix A to Instructions for Form 1023 *(Revised June 2006)*, available at www.irs.gov/pub/irs-pdf/i1023.pdf (last visited Feb. 7, 2011).

[187] Queen of Angels Hospital v. Younger, 136 Cal. Rptr. 36, 42-43 (Cal. Ct. App. 1977).

[188] Stern v. Lucy Webb Hayes National Training School for Deaconesses & Missionaries, 381 F. Supp 1003, 1013-17 (D.D.C. 1974).

[189] Rev. Ruling 69-545, 1969-2 C.B. 117.

[190] IRC § 501(c)(3).

[191] IRC § 511.

[192] *In re* Manhattan Eye, Ear and Throat Hosp., 715 N.Y.S. 2d 575 (1999).

[193] *Id.* at 593 (citation omitted).

[194] IRC § 501(c)(3). There are tax exemptions for other types of non-profit corporations, but because of the tax exemption and deductibility of contributions, the IRS focuses scrutiny on charities.

[195] IRC § 4958(f)(1).

[196] IRC § 4958(c)(1).

[197] *See* Internal Revenue Service, Form 4720 Instructions, available at www.irs.gov/pub/irs-pdf/i4720.pdf (last visited Feb. 7, 2011).

[198] IRC § 4958.

[199] Treasury Reg. § 53.4958-6(a)(3).

[200] *See, e.g.,* Tex. Civ. Prac. & Rem. § 84.

[201] ABA Coordinating Committee on Non-profit Governance, *Guide to Non-profit Corporate Governance in the Wake of Sarbanes-Oxley*, 2 (2005).

[202] *Id.*

203 The IRS offers Form 990 Resources and Tools for Exempt Organizations online at www.irs.gov/charities/article/0,,id=214269,00.html (last visited Feb. 7, 2011).

204 Catalyst, *2009 Catalyst Census: Fortune 500 Women Board Directors*, available at www.catalyst.org/file/320/2010_fortune_500_census_ women_board_directors.pdf (last visited Feb. 7, 2011).

205 *Id.* at Appendix 3, available at www.catalyst.org/etc/Census_app/09US/ 2009_Fortune_500_Census_Appendix_3.pdf (last visited Feb. 7, 2011).

206 *Id.* at Appendix 2, available at www.catalyst.org/etc/Census_app/09US/ 2009_Fortune_500_Census_Appendix_2.pdf (last visited Feb. 7, 2011).

207 ION, *Guys Who Get It: Business Leaders Who Understand the Value of Diversity at the Top, The 6th Annual Status Report of Women Directors and Executive Officers of Public Companies in Fourteen Regions of the United States*, 11 (Mar. 2010) (quoting TK Kerstetter).

208 *Id.*

209 Wellesley Centers for Women, *Critical Mass on Corporate Boards: Why Three or More Women Enhance Governance*, 37 (2006).

210 *Id.* at 34.

211 *Id.* at v.

212 Catalyst, *The Bottom Line: Connecting Corporate Performance and Women's Representation on Boards* (2007), available at www.catalyst.org/ (last visited Oct. 2, 2007).

213 David Carter, Betty Simkins & W. Gary Simpson, Corporate Governance, Board Diversity, and Firm Value, *The Financial Review*, Vol 38, p. 33-53 (2003).

214 Catalyst, *2010 Catalyst Census: Fortune 500 Women Board Directors*, available at www.catalyst.org/publication/460/2010-catalyst-census-for-tune-500-women-board-directors (last visited June 12, 2011).

215 Lois Joy, *Advancing Women Leaders: The Connection Between Women Board Directors and Women Corporate Officers* (July 2008), available at www.catalyst.org (last visited Feb. 7, 2011).

216 Catalyst, 2010 Catalyst Census: Fortune 500Women Board Directors. http://www.catalyst.org/publication/460/2010-catalyst-census-fortune-500-women-board-directors

[217]   Spencer Stuart, *2010 Spencer Stuart Board Index*, 17.

[218]   Dennis C. Carey & Nayla Rizk, *Spencer Stuart Governance Letter: Seismic Shift in Board Competition* (Third Quarter 2005).

[219]   Spencer Stuart, *2010 Spencer Stuart Board Index*, 5.

[220]   Theodore Dysart, Board Trends for 2006: It's Back to the Future, *Heidrick & Struggles Governance Letter,* 63 (2005).

[221]   Carey & Rizk, *supra* note 218.

[222]   *Id.* at 38.

[223]   *Id.* at 49.

[224]   Catalyst, *2010 Catalyst Census of Women Corporate Officers* (2010), available at www.catalyst.org (last visited Feb. 7, 2011).

[225]   Spencer Stuart, *2010 Spencer Stuart Board Index*, 5.

[226]   Spencer Stuart, *2010 Spencer Stuart Board Index*, 31.

[227]   Catalyst, *2010 Catalyst Census of Women Corporate Officers* (2010), available at www.catalyst.org (last visited Feb. 7, 2011).

[228]   Spencer Stuart, *2010 Spencer Stuart Board Index*, 31.

[229]   Spencer Stuart, *2010 Spencer Stuart Board Index*, 15.

[230]   National Association of Corporate Directors, *2005 Public Governance Survey*, 2 (2005).

[231]   SEC Press Release, *SEC Approves Enhanced Disclosure About Risk, Compensation and Corporate Governance* (Dec. 16, 2009), available at www.sec.gov/news/press/2009/2009-268.htm. *See also* www.sec.gov/rules/final/2009/33-9089.pdf.

[232]   *Id.*

[233]   Office of State Treasurer Denise Nappier, Bringing Diversity to the Boardroom: Connecticut's Unique Partnership, available at www.state.ct.us/ott/pressreleases/press2002/pr101502.pdf (last visited Aug. 2006).

[234]   The Calvert Group, Ltd., *Calvert and State of Connecticut Successfully Advocate for Diversity at Netflix,* available at www.calvert.com/newsarticle.html?article=16590 (last visited June 28, 2011).

[235] ION, *Guys Who Get It: Business Leaders Who Understand the Value of Diversity at the Top: The 6th Annual Status Report of Women Directors and Executive Officers of Public Companies in Fourteen Regions of the United States,* available at www.ionwomen.org (last visited February 14, 2011).

[236] Catalyst, *2006 Catalyst Census of Women Corporate Officers* (2007), available at www.catalyst.org (last visited Feb. 14, 2011).

[237] United States Department of Health and Human Services, Office of Inspector General & American Health Lawyers Association, *An Integrated Approach to Corporate Compliance: A Resource for Health Care Organization Boards of Directors* (July 1, 2004).

[238] Wellesley Centers for Women, *supra* note 209, 51.

Index

This index is not intended to be 100% comprehensive. Instead, it provides page numbers and reference points for some key topics that the reader may be interested in learning more about.

Order more copies of Answering the Call!

Did you enjoy this book? If so, consider purchasing an extra copy, or buying another copy:

- As a gift for a new board member looking for an introduction to board service.
- For a colleague you are mentoring who should be considering board service as a professional growth opportunity.
- As a set for your director colleagues.
- For a friend or colleague who needs encouragement to consider board service.
- For your company's nominating committee chair—has he or she considered including at least three women on your company's board of directors?
- All proceeds from this book benefit the WBL Foundation.

ANSWERING THE CALL:
Understanding the Duties, Risks, and Rewards of Corporate Governance (Fourth Edition)

AUTHORS:
Lynn Shapiro Snyder, Esq. and Robert D. Reif, Esq.

Publication Date: 2011
Paperback; $24.95, 191 pages
ISBN-13: 978-0-9797557-2-9

To order, visit www.wbl.org or Amazon.com